Tales from the Police Locker room Vol. 1

Perry P. Rose

with

Joan Nelson

Art Copyright © Stephen Huggett 1993

Cover Photo - Impulse Photography
Calgary, Alberta

Edited by Laurie Anne Witwer

Printed in Canada

Canadian Cataloguing in Publication Data

Rose, Perry P. (Perry Paul), 1948-
Tales from the police locker room

Vol.1
ISBN 0-9697756-5-2 (v. 1)

1. Police--Ancedotes. 2. Police--Humor.
I. Nelson, Joan, 1939- II. Title.
  PN6231.P59R69 1996   363.2'0207
  C96-910715-3

For information contact:

WORDSTORM PRODUCTIONS INC.,
PO BOX 49132, 7740 - 18 ST SE,
CALGARY, ALBERTA, CANADA T2C 3W5

or:

WORDSTORM PRODUCTIONS INC.,
1520 - 3 ST. N.W. C-104
GREAT FALLS, MONTANA, USA 59404

Published by Wordstorm Productions Inc.
Quality Paperback
First Printing October 1993
Second Printing November 1993
Third Printing January 1994
Fourth Printing August 1994
Fifth Printing January 1995
Trade Paperback
First Printing October 1996

This book is dedicated to the

men and women of the

CALGARY POLICE SERVICE

who made it possible.

Thank you for your good humour.

The laughter of police officers

may not be the presentation

of true emotions.

To laugh may be to cry.

OFFICE of the CHIEF of POLICE
CALGARY, CANADA

FORWARD

Being a police officer in today's society is a challenging and, at times, stress filled career. Whether its investigating a crime, taking control at the scene of a traffic accident, or providing information to a member of the public, people expect officers to be calm, authoritative and highly professional.

The police officer's public persona is balanced by a long tradition of humour. Having the ability to talk about a difficult situation with your colleagues and see the light moments, or to recount a humorous conversation or predicament is part of the team work all police officers need in order to do their jobs well.

Tales from the Police Locker Room, by Perry Rose and Joan Nelson, captures many fine examples of police humour. No doubt, some of these stories have been embellished somewhat as they have made their rounds. But, they accurately portray a side of policing the public rarely gets to see.

G. Borbridge
CHIEF OF POLICE

316 - 7TH Avenue S.E., Calgary, Alberta T2G 0J2

INTRODUCTION

Armed with truth and justice, the city's finest hit the streets day in and day out "To serve and protect." Confident these enforcers of the law are the protectors of life, limb and property, citizens go about their daily routines steadfast in the knowledge that their police service is ready to spring into action any time, any place, in the continuing battle against crime and/or evil!

When the call for help goes out, John and Mary Q. Citizen watch in awe as the darting police cruiser is deftly manoeuvred to its destination. They admire the flashing lights and wailing siren, sometimes secretly yearning to be in the driver's seat.

But what's really happening inside the

swift patrol car flitting through traffic like a gnat on a summer's night? Let's take a closer look! The officer just left a 7-Eleven store with a giant grape slurpy. A few blocks down the road a lady thought she heard someone trying to break into her house. The call was dispatched and help was on the way.

The constable started his car and deftly flicked on the emergency equipment. Balancing the slurpy in one hand, he dropped the transmission into drive and exited the parking lot. Over the curb and into the traffic he fled, holding the slurpy cup just right so as not to spill a single drop. While driving he also had to answer the radio, signal his turns, blow the horn, turn the wheels and wave at the kid on the corner who would have been devastated for life if the nice policeman had not waved back.

Soon he arrived at the house in question and pulled up in front. As he got out of the car he realized that he must leave the grape slurpy behind. He smiled with great satisfaction as he comprehended the tremendous feat he had just accomplished by responding to this call without spilling a single drop. He reached back into the vehicle and placed the waxed cup on the dashboard. It fit nicely and he stood back. Flicking the lock down he closed the car door, and as he turned away he heard a dull thud behind him. He looked over his shoulder to see his grape slurpy, all super-size of it, bounce off the steering wheel and splatter all over the driver's seat.

The call turned out to be a "no cause." The lady heard a tree knocking against the wall in the wind, nothing more. Her problems were over, but the officer's were just beginning. The front seat was a pretty grape colour. He humbly asked the nice lady for some newspaper. With a question in her eye she brought him the sports section, thinking he must be bored or maybe couldn't afford his own paper. He thanked her and returned to the patrol car. Placing the paper onto the front seat he slid in, squirmed a little, and humbly drove away with icy purple slurpy soaking into his pants, skivvies and cheeks.

After what seemed like an eternity, and a cold one at that, the district police station came into view and he said to himself, "Thank God! I may come out of this unscathed yet, except for frostbite of the arse ... in July!"

He pulled into the back parking lot near the vacuum and exited the vehicle. As he bent over to reach for the now empty slurpy cup, the station door burst open and twenty-five Cub Scouts on an office tour filed out. Of course, the last kid in line had to ask the tour guide, "Is it part of the procedure for cops to wear the sports pages on their butts?"

Ah yes, the life of a policeman, full of intrigue, excitement and danger. But danger doesn't always come in the form of a bad guy. Sometimes it's a little closer to home than you think.

A constable was working one evening with a new partner. They were asked to help in removing a drunken patron from a local bar and were in the process of doing so when the man decided enough was enough. He was going back inside. The fight was on! In the midst of the melée the guy threw his head backwards and butted one of the officers on the left side of his face. In response his partner drew back a fist and attempted to strike the man. This guy wasn't as drunk as they thought and he rather deftly dodged the punch. The arresting officer wasn't so lucky. His partner caught him a full blow on the right cheek with such force he had to let go of the bad guy. The stunned policeman vaguely remembered staggering into the front of the police car and falling over the push bumpers.

Later that shift the daring crew spotted a vehicle on fire and dashed to the rescue. A lady, standing beside her van, was screaming, "My boyfriend is still inside!!" Swashbuckling rescuer number one raced to the driver's door and flung it open. The smoke was thick and black and he had to lean into the compartment to feel for the victim. The stench of burning upholstery bellowed out when his partner tossed open the passenger door. As the rescuer bent forward he heard the distinct hiss of a discharging fire extinguisher from the other side of the van. Whooommphh! He took it full force square in the chest. He stepped back from the now smouldering vehicle looking like a double for the Pilsbury Dough Boy.

As you can see, there is another complete face to police work, a side which the public does not often view. Most officers suffer these humble lessons in the quiet of an alley or in the privacy of their police cars. But now they have come out of the closet and are here to tell the other, more humorous and human, side of police work.

These are the tales you always wanted to hear. These are the stories of the men and women who protect you day and night. These are the allegedly true stories of the royal messes and mistakes, the police bloopers. These are the **TALES FROM THE POLICE LOCKER ROOM VOL. 1.**

CHAPTER ONE

"A policeman's lot is not a happy one," wrote Gilbert and Sullivan. Obviously they had never been exposed to the antics of our city's finest as they patrol the streets in search of crime and/or evil. Humour is a leveller. It knows not race, creed, colour, religious conviction or rank. It can strike, and usually does, at the most inopportune times, leaving in its wake policemen and citizens reduced to gut-laughing, side-holding, tear-streaming fools who are temporarily unable to utter anything more challenging than a one syllable word.

I stopped a truck driver who really had guts. While he was getting his papers for me to write the ticket, he leaned out the window and asked me, "Do you know what the difference is between a porcupine and a police car?"

I had my suspicions but I had to ask.

"No, but I think you're going to tell me, aren't you?"

"Well," he said with a grin, "a porcupine has the pricks on the outside."

I've logged hundreds of miles out of that joke because that's really the way some people see us.

Another fellow once asked me, "What's two hundred feet long and has an asshole at both ends?"

Falling right into the trap I replied, "I don't know."

"A Check Stop," he said as he drove away.

Now, I wouldn't suggest trying these on the next police officer who stops you, but there are other methods which he may find amusing.

Early one Sunday morning I was following a car that was travelling very fast. I decided to stop this person to see what the big hurry was. I activated the emergency equipment and the car pulled over quickly. As I approached the driver I noticed a rather flustered woman reaching for her purse.

"Good morning, ma'am," I said. "May I see your driver's licence, please?"

The woman was obviously not herself because she reached into her purse, pulled out a pair of panties, and passed them to me. As I stared in disbelief, she realized what she had done and quickly stuffed them back into the purse. She turned to me with a horrified lookand blurted, "These aren't the ones I'm wearing ... I mean I have some on ... and a bra ... these are extras ... why am I telling you this ...?"

"I'm not sure," I replied, "but if this is what I get when I ask you for your driver's licence, I hesitate to ask for your insurance and registration. Please slow down and have a nice day."

I love my job and sometimes it loves me back. Sometimes it makes complete fools out of my cohorts and me. We, the members of the Calgary Police Service, now willingly share with you our most intimate, memorable and completely ridiculous moments on the job.

Constable Perry P. Rose

***

I was just out of classes and on the street for a week. My partner and I were dispatched to an industrial accident. An old fellow had been on top of a forklift in a factory and was using an air hose to clean off the tops of the pipes. The guy driving the lift was backing up. The driver was watching the old guy, but didn't see the heater hanging from the roof and backed the forks right into it.

The worker fell like a rag doll onto the cement floor and was pretty badly hurt. Now you have to realize, I was just out of police college, a highly trained professional. I had training in CPR, life saving, and comforting the injured. I was ready to spring into action.

The poor guy landed, more or less, shoulder and left ear first on the floor. He wasn't in good shape. We got there ahead of the ambulance, but like I said, I was a highly trained professional. There were a bunch of people gathered around him, and he was propped up against a wall looking past us with the thousand-yard stare. He was not well.

I walked right over to him and knelt down beside him. I put my hand on his shoulder to comfort him like they taught us in the police college.

I asked him, "Are you all right? Are you okay?"

He was obviously in pain and not

responding to my sympathetic touch or questions. He looked at me with agony in his eyes and gave a terrible moan, mumbling something I couldn't understand.

I leaned forward to better hear him when I felt someone tapping on my shoulder. I turned around to see what he wanted and one of his co-workers said, "He's trying to tell you you're standing on his fingers."

***

It was our last of six night shifts in a row. Both my partner and I were bagged. We had been to court during the previous day and neither of us had had much sleep. Our shift ended at 0700 hours and we had only forty-five minutes left. We couldn't wait to put the car away and go home, but as always happens, we were sent to a minor fender bender which was blocking the beginnings of rush hour traffic.

We pulled up to the scene located at a very busy intersection and sorted out the drivers. We put both of them into the back seat of the police car and had them begin writing their accident statements. My partner and I were both doing the required forms in the front seat. Suddenly, I realized that I had dozed off, but I had no idea for how long. I opened my right eye a crack and looked to see if my partner had noticed. He hadn't - he was sound asleep too! I reached over and gave him a little nudge. He woke up with a snort and quickly wiped the drool from the corner of his mouth. I turned to the two drivers as if nothing had happened and asked them if they were finished with their statements.

"Yes we did," said the one fellow, "quite some time ago. What were you two doing up there, thinking about whom to charge?"

"Uh, yes, of course, that's it," I said. "Sometimes these things take a lot of consideration."

To this day I have no idea how long we were asleep.

***

I was on impaired driver detail with a female partner one night and we spotted a car weaving all over the road. We followed behind him for a bit and then activated the emergency equipment to pull him over. As far as he was concerned we didn't exist. We gave him a shot or two on the siren - he just ignored us. We followed him a few more blocks and he finally stopped right in front of his house.

As we pulled in behind him he suddenly bolted from the car and started walking very quickly up the front walk.

My partner jumped out of the car and yelled, "Stop, police!"

He just kept on walking and didn't even let on he heard her. She ran after him and cut across the lawn. Well, it had rained a little and the grass was wet. I looked over and there she was, running up the slope on the grass but not going anywhere. You know, like the little guy in the cartoon, feet just a flyin' but no forward steam. I started to laugh and got out of the car.

I thought I should cut the driver off at the pass, so I ran up the next lawn and burst through the hedge like the Incredible Hulk. I sized him up and he looked pretty big.

I figured, "I'll football tackle him and hold him until may partner gets up the slope." He didn't even see me coming, and by the time I got to him my partner had regained her traction. She was just about to grab him.

I hit him pretty hard with my shoulder and he went down like a dishrag. All three of us fell in a heap and he landed on top of my partner, face up. She was on her back with her legs wrapped around his waist. He still refused to be arrested and rolled over onto his hands and knees.

My partner held on tight and came up

riding him horsy-back style across the lawn, yelling, "Stop, you're under arrest!"

I just wanted to get him into the car and get the hell out of there before the neighbours woke up and saw us.

***

While on patrol late one night I spotted a vehicle travelling with its lights out in a high crime area. We had been hit heavily in the recent past and had been requested to stop and check any cars in the location that appeared to be involved in criminal activity. Driving through an industrial centre at 2:00 a.m. with your lights out is usually a good sign that you don't want to be seen by the police or anyone else.

Slipping the police car in behind the suspect vehicle, I followed for a block or two in an attempt to determine if the driver was in the area on legitimate business. He drove into a parking lot and the vehicle disappeared behind a darkened building.

"This may be it," I thought to myself. "I may have the guy responsible for these B and E's."

I turned the lights off on my police cruiser and coasted up behind the suspect. Using the element of surprise, I hit all the switches at the same time, turning on the high beams, take-down floodlights, and the overhead emergency lights. I bounded out of the car and approached the suspect, flashlight in hand. As I reached the side of his car, he rolled the window down and I demanded of him, "What's your name?"

The gentleman of Southeast Asian descent replied with a phrase that resounded distinctly of "Fuck You!"

I reached in through the window and grabbed him by the shirt. "Don't you talk to me like that!" I yelled.

The driver, now appearing quite shaken, pulled his licence from his shirt pocket and held it up to my anger-flushed face.

"No, no!" he cried. "That my name ... Phouc Huu!"

***

One evening while on patrol on the M11 motorway in England, where it is, by the way, illegal to stop for any reason, my partner and I spied a car stopped on the shoulder. We pulled up and looked around, but there was no one there. Then we saw a gentleman coming up the bank near the car. My partner got out and said to him, "Having problems, sir?"

"Well, Officer," the man replied, "I saw

you stop, but I was looking for the nearest shit house."

With that my partner reached into his breast pocket, pulled out his ticket book and said, "You've found him."

***

In England it is illegal to arrest anybody for drinking and driving before you demand a breath sample for testing. If you do so, you have an unlawful arrest. I, being a rookie, arrested a man and then demanded a breath sample from him. He refused and was then conveyed to the office where he identified himself to the charging sergeant as a lawyer. He demanded a pencil and paper to write down his own notes as to the unlawful arrest. After placing him in a cell with his paper and pencil, I explained to the sergeant what I had done.

He quickly sent me out onto the street to stop the Grimsby Fish delivery man who passed by our office daily. He instructed me to arrange for a flat of kippers, which I did. I was puzzled. I thought maybe the sergeant was going to treat us all to breakfast. When I went back inside, he sent me to the linen cupboard to acquire six bedsheets. He recruited

Tales from the Police Locker room Vol. I

four other officers and led us in a parade down to where the lawyer was busy writing. The sergeant had us don the sheets, which we could see out of, and put our helmets on back to front. He then armed each of us with a fresh kipper and we entered the cell.

The sergeant led us in a ring-a-rosie dance around the man, and when we came to the end of each verse, we tapped him lightly with a kipper. When the song was done we left the room.

The lawyer appeared in court the next morning for his hearing and read his story verbatim to the judge. When he reached the part about the sheets, kippers and nursery rhyme, the judge stopped him.

He said, "It is quite obvious to the court, sir, that you were very intoxicated when this fine constable stopped you. I find you guilty and suggest you curtail your drinking habits."

***

I was in court one day for a traffic matter and another officer was giving evidence. The defence lawyer asked him, "This offence occurred at night, did it not?"

The officer responded, "Yes it did."

"Was it dark?" asked the lawyer.

The officer replied, "Well, yeah, it was night."

"And," continued the lawyer, "did you have your lights on?"

"Yes I did," said the officer, "and so did your client."

"And just how far were you behind my client at the time of this incident?"

"Oh," the constable scratched his head a moment, "'bout two hundred feet I s'pose."

"Two hundred feet's rather a long way at night, wouldn't you agree, constable?" asked the lawyer with a wry smile.

"Two hundred feet's rather a long way in the day time too," said the constable.

Not to be beaten the lawyer continued his attack, "Exactly, officer, night time, two hundred feet behind my client. Now let me ask you this: How far can you see at night?"

"Well," said the officer, "on a clear night, sir, I can see the moon. How far is that?"

***

At the Calgary Exhibition & Stampede grounds there is a tunnel that goes under the grandstand to the infield. I was with my very senior partner at the time, and we were patrolling the park. It was spring and the water in the tunnel was still frozen over. As we were driving through we noticed the ceiling getting very close to the overhead lights on the car. Trained investigators that we were, we quickly figured out that the ice was not level.

We decided we should get out of there and my partner drove quickly to the far end. We forgot that the tip of the tunnel had been in sunlight most of the day. Just as I opened my mouth to speak, there was a great roar and the ice gave way under us. The car sunk to the door handles in a flash. My agile part ner climbed out through his window onto the roof without collecting a single drop of water. By the time I got my seatbelt undone the water was up to my chest and cold.

I remember thinking, "My nuts'll be shrunk for a month and I'm gonna get electrocuted. All the damned wiring is under water and so am I!"

I shot up through the window like a wet bar of soap in a shower, checking for sparks and cursing my partner.

"1134 to dispatch, can we have a tow truck to the Stampede tunnel," he said quietly into his portable radio. It was, of course, in vain, and in minutes every free police car in the city was at our location.

As we were being pulled from the icy grave by the tow truck winch my partner yelled to our fellow officers, "Okay, listen up! We need a rrreallly good story for the sarge. Best submission gets a month's free donuts!"

***

I was assigned to crowd control at a huge fire downtown. It was a bitterly cold night, about twenty-five below zero. All the water the fire department was pouring into the building was gushing onto the road and freezing in layers. There were thrill seekers standing everywhere. Some of them even tried to walk right past the front of the burning structure. It was my job to make sure they didn't get too close.

An old wino walked by me and I called to him, "Hey, cross the street and walk over there."

He wouldn't listen to me and was getting really close to the fire. I reached for him and missed. When my hand got about two inches from him he slipped on the ice and fell face-first with a great skidding splash into the pool of water. The water froze on him instantly. By the time I got him up he looked like a relic from the ice age.

Of course, the biggest guy in the crowd yelled at me, "Hey, leave the old guy alone! Why don't you pick on somebody my size!!"

Not wanting to take this behemoth on

in front of everyone, and probably lose, I yelled back what I had heard so many people say on my job, "I didn't do it! I didn't do it!"

I rarely believe that when I hear it, and the multitude didn't either. So much for credibility in the crowd control department.

***

I was in Mounted Patrol and was riding my horse along the pedestrian section of our downtown mall. We had just been ordered to wear riding helmets and I hated them. They were hot and heavy and I detested putting them on. A fight broke out in front of me in the midst of a pretty big crowd, and when one of the guys saw me he took off. I rode up to the other fellow to find out what was happening. While I was talking to him the offender came back and hit him again ... right in front of me!

I leaned over on the horse, grabbed the idiot by the front of his shirt, and lifted him off the ground.

I was going to tell him, "Listen fella, don't be doing this again or you're going to jail!"

As I pulled him upwards my helmet dropped forward over my eyes, blinding me, and I accidentally head-butted him. I knocked him out cold, and when I let go he fell right by the horse's feet.

I could hear people in the crowd saying, "Wow, that guy fainted. He must really be scared of the police!"

***

I was walking the beat downtown when my partner and I stopped to check out a known drug dealer. We pulled him into a washroom in a cafe and did a strip search on him in a toilet stall. He was standing nude on the toilet tank because he didn't want to put his feet on the bathroom floor. When I went to pass him back his clothes the toilet lid slipped, and he started break dancing on top of the tank to keep his balance. He missed the bundle and they fell into the toilet bowl. As I leaned over to get them he tried to kick me in the face, so I grabbed for his foot and missed. A bathroom stall was no place to be waltzing with a druggie. I lost my balance and fell forward, driving one arm into the bowl and flushing the toilet with the other as I went. Everything except his jeans went down. I extricated myself from between the tank and the wall and passed the soaking wet pants to him with my night stick.

"Thanks a bunch!" was all he said.

***

I was dispatched to a call about a woman who had locked herself out of her apartment. It was transmitted as a woman in her bra and panties at a phone booth. When I arrived, sure enough, there she was in a black bra and panties.

I was obtaining the necessary information from her when she finally said, "You know, this city has the most police coverage I've ever seen."

"What do you mean?" I asked.

She replied, "Well, since you got here there have been at least twenty police cars drive by."

***

I was working with a rookie and we had just become involved into our first chase with a stolen car. I was driving and it was his job to give the description, direction of travel, etc., to the dispatcher. When you get into a chase the adrenalin pumps out pretty good, you speak too fast and your voice goes up a few notches in pitch. The poor rookie was trying to give the info to the dispatcher, but he was running everything together so badly that she couldn't make him out.

She waited for a break in his transmission and then said to him, "Okay, okay, just slow down."

He looked at me blankly and said, "They want you to slow down."

***

I recall one lazy summer afternoon when my radar alarm was triggered. I bolted from the police car and stopped a large vehicle that was not only speeding, but was being driven with one set of wheels on the sidewalk. As I got near the car I noticed a huge tropical bird sitting on the headrest behind the driver.

The gentleman rolled his window down and blurted out, "I'm sorry officer, but my parrot has diarrhea!"

I looked over the top of my sunglasses at the guy with a smile and replied, "Can't say that I blame him the way you were driving. May I see your license please?"

***

The burglar alarm had never been a good one before, so why should it be any different this time? We responded in our usual manner to the building at Heritage Park. For those who don't know, Heritage Park is a rebuilt old western town complete with hotels, jails, train stations and houses.

The alarm was coming from a main building in the downtown part and we drove to within a block where we got out on foot. I took the boardwalk and my partner went around the back to check doors. As I came to the corner of the building something moved on the street. I stuck my head around but I couldn't see anything. I stepped onto the sidewalk, and out of the corner of my eye I saw a guy with a gun pointed right at me.

In a flash I twisted and drew down on him, yelling, "Police, drop the gun!"

As I turned to face him I saw he wasn't going to drop it. The weapon was pointed right at my chest.

Without a second thought I fired three rounds and hit him square in the upper torso. To my amazement he didn't go down. I was ready to squeeze off three more rounds when my partner came running around the corner with his gun out, calling for back-up.

He took one look and burst out laughing. "Nice goin' hotshot," he said. "You just blew away the Western Outfitter's mannequin."

***

My rookie partner had been making comments for a few weeks about how senior policemen were cynical and didn't give a damn.

I thought, "I'll just show you when I get the chance, fella."

A few days later we were driving through our patrol area and I saw a little puppy on the sidewalk.

I said to myself, "Self, here's your chance."

I opened the car door and called the pup over. It came right to me and climbed onto my lap. The poor thing was all muddy, but that was all right because I was going to be caring and compassionate and show this wet-behind-the-ears rook a thing or two. I looked on the dog's collar and it read "Muffy," with a phone number.

As we drove away I contacted the dispatcher and had her do a reverse on the phone number so we could return the puppy to its owner. While we were driving around waiting for the address to come back, I was really getting my licks in with the rookie. I was telling him just how understanding and compassionate we could be as we "matured" on the job. I was really laying it on thick, describing to him how there's a poor little girl out there somewhere who is crying because her puppy is gone, and how happy she will be when the thoughtful policeman returns her dog to her. I would be her hero!

Dispatch finally came back with the address and I had to pull out the map to find it. We had been driving around so much I was a little confused as to how to get to the place. We drove onto the street and the rookie started calling out house numbers. I was ready to make my big debut with a sad little girl.

When we finally reached the house, I looked out and we were right in front of the place where I had scooped the dog. There, in the window ... crying her heart out ... was this poor little girl. She had watched the police come and take her dog away!

***

One night we were sitting near the railway yards at about midnight when the workers get off shift. Quite often the wives or girlfriends of these guys would pick them up there. Right across the street from us was a gas station and a girl decided that she needed to go for a pee. She went in behind the building by some old tires and dropped her pants to her ankles.

Through the glass bay windows the garage was in darkness. Inside was a great big German Shepherd, and I guess he took exception to her being on the property. Just as she got to about the middle of her pee, the dog lunged into the window, snarling and snapping at her, nearly popping the pane out onto her lap. The poor girl came around the corner squealing and screaming, pulling up her pants and trying to run at the same time. We thought she'd been attacked by somebody so we jumped out of the car and ran to her. We got there and she yelled out the story. I was already laughing, but now I really lost it. You know, maintaining a professional image at all times!

She gave me a blast, so I settled down and bit my lip a few times. About then her boyfriend arrived and saw her standing in the parking lot with two policemen while she was pulling up her pants. He came running over to see what was going on and she told him the story. He burst out laughing and I lost it again.

In the middle of this she gave us both supreme hell and yelled, "This is not funny!" Her boyfriend and I stopped, looked at each other, screamed, and said in unison, "Oh-ho-ho, yes it is!"

CHAPTER TWO

Well, is your funny bone oiled up yet?
That was only the beginning and there's plenty
more where that came from. Oh, by the way,
this is Joan now, Perry is taking a breather. I
work in CPIC as a supervisor. That's the area
where the constables call in for names to be
checked for warrants or records, and all the
other mysterious, technical business we
perform so well. Contrary to popular belief,
CPIC stands for Canadian Police Information
Centre, not Calgary Police Introduction
Centre. However, some romantic matches have
been born in the CPIC area between the
operators and the police members. Do the
civilians working for the police department
have their days too? You bet your life!

We deal with the street policemen on a
daily basis and get to know them quite well.
When they come to headquarters to obtain
information many frivolous exchanges take

place between us, running the gamut from jokes, to family pictures, to stories about the men's vasectomies. (For some reason we seem to hear about every vasectomy on the department, but not much about the forty hours of labour the wife went through before she made him have the damn vasectomy.)

The Calgary Police Service used to host an annual basketball tournament. It was more of a time for parties and dancing than basketball, and the guys were there to "play" for the most part. It was a scream to watch them stagger onto the court in the morning. Have you ever seen someone dribble when they're hungover? ... a basketball I mean! The referee had to be very careful when blowing his whistle too or he would have found it lodged in some other wind-producing orifice of his body!

I was working with a woman who was helping with the tournament. It was lunch time, and a couple of the CPIC operators had gone, leaving just the two of us to work the area. A call came in from one of the car crews and she finished processing their request. As she terminated the transmission, she turned to me and began discussing the upcoming tournament. The conversation commenced as a discussion about the tournament, but quickly deteriorated into verbal carnage, with the two of us discussing the players rather than the plays. We continued with comments and innuendo about how we were going to be scoring during the time and above all keeping score - even something about helping the cuter guys dribble their balls.

My final comment to her was, "Well, I certainly hope you don't come to me in four months and ask for maternity leave!"

We were in the midst of roaring laughter when we suddenly heard a tiny, lilting voice over the radio saying, "Oh Records ... your mike is stuck open ... and has been for the past ten minutes ..."

Our jaws dropped. Every police car in the city on that channel had heard every word we said. To this day the only buns we discuss at work are dinner buns!

Policemen are very nice people and will go out of their way to help you. I remember one cold, windy day, I was walking towards headquarters on my way to work when a car crew spotted me. Gentlemen that they were, they offered me a ride which I gratefully accepted. Instead of taking me to the back door, they pulled right up in front of headquarters on a street that was forbidden to police vehicles.

As we made a u-turn the one fellow said to me, "With our luck the chief will be standing out front. I wonder what he'd do to us? Now let me show you how much of a gentleman I really am."

He jumped from the vehicle, and with

great flourish pulled open my door, bowing deeply as I stepped from the car. I never got to thank him. The poor officer stood up to come face-to-face with the chief. He tore so many strips of skin off the constable's back he doesn't have enough left to close his eyes on night shift now.

I've been collecting stories for years, and when I first started I knew I wanted to put them into book form. Somehow, a radio announcer in Calgary got wind of my idea, and invited me to be on his show. I was thrilled with the idea and gladly accepted. One of the things he asked me to explain was how I went about collecting stories. What I tried to tell him was that I had a Christmas party at my house every year and would invite policemen and their wives over for homemade eggnog. When they became relaxed they would tell me quite a few of the stories. Well, you know how things in the media have a habit of changing. It came out that I liked to invite policemen to my place for a few drinks and get them loaded so they would tell me stories. Wrong! Guys! Don't get any ideas!!

Over the years I have been blessed with stories provided by everyone from rookies to the chief. No one has escaped my ever-listening ear ... so read on, faithful, as the women and men in blue continue to exhibit their skill, daring do ... and in some cases ... their daring don't.   Joan Nelson

It was an injury accident. We happened to see the rollover right in front of us. A drunken driver clipped the rear end of a lady's car and flipped it onto its roof. I'd say the total ages of the occupants of the rolled vehicle had to be well over three hundred years and there were only four of them inside.

One of the elderly ladies was thrown from the car and had a broken pelvis. Now, you have to realize that this is on a major thoroughfare at four o'clock in the afternoon. Traffic backed up from asshole to breakfast time in an instant. All the emergency vehicles arrived, and half the population of southeast Calgary was there watching.

The poor old lady was in great pain, but there were two firemen, a paramedic and myself with her. We were going to lift her up onto a stretcher and the onlookers pushed in closer to see. As I bent over to pick her up the ass of my pants ripped out, right from my belt all the way around to my zipper. My hands were full so I couldn't cover up.

I could hear people behind me go "Ooo-ahh".

It took forever to get her onto the stretcher. Yes Mom, I was wearing clean underwear, thank God! I stood up, straightened my tie (for lack of anything better to do), then shuffled backwards to the police car where I glued myself to the front seat.

About three months later we attended court over the accident. My partner was the first called to give evidence. He was on the stand quite a while and I was in the back room where the witnesses go so they can't hear the evidence before it's their turn. When the court clerk came back to call me she was smiling ... no, grinning was more like it.

I thought, "Well, this is nice. At least everyone is in a good mood in there."

When I walked into the courtroom the entire place erupted in laughter, the judge, the prosecutor, the defence, gallery clerks, everybody, even the damned prisoner. I looked in the back row and there was my partner hiding behind his hat. The son-of-a bitch told them everything. To this day when I see that judge he still chuckles.

***

I was working traffic detail alone one sunny day when a car went zipping past me on the main drag. I pulled in behind it and got a good clock for a charge. After a few blocks I hit the emergency equipment and the driver pulled over. I noticed that a young lady was driving, and as I walked closer I saw that she was quite attractive. I approached the car window with an impressive air of professionalism and leaned over to ask her for her licence. As I opened my mouth to speak, the left lens fell out of my sunglasses. Plink! Stooping over to pick it up I struck my forehead on the car mirror. By now the lady was holding her hand over her mouth, unable to decide if she should risk laughter or not. As I stood up and removed the remnants of my sunglasses, a truck went by and blew my hat off. At this point she lost it.

I smiled my most professional smile and said "Please slow down and have a nice day."

I left.

***

When I was attached to the Identification Section I was called to a beautiful house which had been broken into. Upon arrival, I found a very pretty young lady who was the owner of the residence, and I knew this was going to make my day a little brighter. The bad guy had broken a rear window in the basement and climbed into her bedroom, stepping right onto her bed.

About the only thing worth fingerprint ing in the room was her white dresser. I dusted it with no results. The drawer had been opened, so I pulled on it and found a plastic pill box, circular, with the word "Ortho" written on it. I picked it up by the edges so as not to destroy any fingerprints which might have been on it.

The poor girl turned all red and said, "This is so embarrassing."

"Don't be embarrassed," I said to her. "I'm a married man. I've seen birth control pills before."

While I was consoling her I guess I was squeezing the container, and it sprang open with a resounding snap. Instantaneously her folded up diaphragm erupted from the case like a rocket and ricocheted off everything in the room before coming to rest on the floor at her feet.

***

When I was in traffic detail I stopped an impaired driver one night. I was working alone and there were four people in the vehicle. I got out and had the driver get into the back of the police car. I called for a tow truck and was waiting for it to get there when the other three guys decided they were going to help their buddy escape. They all piled out of the car. I saw them coming, so I called for back-

46

"A DRUNK DRIVER BREATHING ON YOU
IS NOT ASSAULT P.O! ...
...... ON SECOND THOUGHT THOUGH."

up. The tow truck arrived just as they got to the police car, and he knew they meant business.

The driver barrelled out of his truck and grabbed a tire iron. By this time I was out of the police car with my night stick and back-up was just arriving. In a matter of seconds we had them all handcuffed and sitting on the grass beside the road.

As I walked past them one of the guys asked quietly, "I suppose it's too late to apologize?"

***

Three guys ran across the street against the light right in front of my police car.

I got on the P.A. system and yelled, "Hey, get back over here and wait for the light!"

Two of them came back, but the third gave us the finger and kept walking. I scrambled out of the car to grab him and my partner followed me. The guy was putting up a bit of a fight, and we were struggling with him when I looked around for the car.

"Where's the damn car?" I yelled.

We peered over our shoulders, and there it was, going down the street all by itself. He'd left it in drive.

My partner ran off after the car and left

me to continue fighting with the bad guy. By the time he got back I was getting a bit tired. I took out my cuffs but the guy was all arms and legs. I saw a bare wrist and slammed the cuffs hard onto it. GGrrriithcchh!

"Gotcha!" I yelled.

In my ear I heard my partner's voice in agony, "You stupid son-of-a-bitch, that's my wrist!"

***

Not much happens on some night shifts, so you find yourself driving around looking for something to do. It was about two o'clock in the morning and we saw a small group gathered on the side of the road. We thought we had better investigate, so we pulled over and stopped.

There was a cat lying on the side of the road and the people were asking, "What are we going to do with this poor thing?"

We decided we had better do something about this, so we got out of the car and looked. The cat was lying there barely twitching.

I thought, "It's almost gone and we can't just leave it. We've got to do something about it."

We looked at each other and asked the silent question, which one of us was going to dispatch the cat? Neither of us wanted to pull out a shotgun and blow it all over the street.

I said to my partner, "I'll get my night stick."

At that time we had those little fourteen-inch truncheons. So I got it from the car and was going to put the poor creature out of its misery. Except, I had never killed a thing on purpose in my life. I decided to hit it on the head behind the ear with a single, well-directed and painless blow.

I knelt over the frail animal and gazed into its fear-filled eyes as I raised the stick to striking position. At the last moment I flinched and the blow glanced off the top of the cat's head. It jumped up, ran about three or four feet and then went down again.

I looked at my partner and said, "This cat isn't dying, it's just injured! What are we going to do now?"

"Let's take it to the animal hospital," he suggested.

All the people were watching as we picked the poor thing up and placed it gently into the trunk of our police car.

When we got to the animal hospital we met a nice lady veterinarian. We laid the cat down gently on the examination table and she began her diagnosis.

She checked it carefully from top to bottom, and then turned to us and said, "There's only one thing wrong with this cat ... it's got a concussion ..."

English court is very formal. They wear white wigs and robes and speak the Queen's English at all times. I was in court one day while attached to Scotland Yard. A bunch of rioters were charged with laying a licking on one of the area cars. They had beaten up the constables and destroyed the police car. The prosecutor was giving his account of the evidence when I arrived. The judge was prim and proper and was watching the proceedings from his bench which was way up on top of the court area.

The prosecutor was pointing and saying, "And aaalll these accuseds here, My Lord, were jumping up and down on the police car. And this accused here ... this ... this accused here bent the police aerial off the back and said, 'That's fucked you 'asn't it' ... Just like that, My Lord, 'That's fucked you 'asn't it!' But it 'adn't fucked them, My Lord, they 'ad their portable radios with them!"

***

I worked on the bomb squad in London with the Yard and we were deep undercover. The squad there is like the surveillance detail here. We were following a suspect one day, and to do it properly, we would use three guys to walk what they called the parallel. We'd be in front of him sometimes or beside him, behind him, wherever we could keep an eye on him. We had the latest state-of-the-art equipment which consisted of a radio earpiece and a separate mouthpiece which was hidden under your watch - the best available. We were all dressed like scum bags - I mean really dirty and filthy. We wanted this guy bad. He had left a case of T.N.T. in front of a department store and it was live - could have killed dozens of people. This was no small time.

All of a sudden the voice of our leader came lilting through the earpiece, "Last one to tap dance is a queer."

I looked behind me to see two undercover policemen dancin' away to beat the band down the sidewalk.

***

One of the things we used to do in England was to get people from off the street for identification parade. You call it a line-up over here. A little old lady's shop had been robbed and we were looking for people to stand in the line. We went out and found five guys in a group.

We thought, "What luck, we don't have to go any further! We have all we need right here."

They agreed and we took them into the line-up room.

We brought the lady to the station and told her, "We want you to go in and 'ave a look. When you come back out you can tell us 'oo you think done it."

So in she went and took a great long look.

When she came out we asked her, "Well, did you see 'im? Did you see the one what done it?"

She said, "No, there's no one there from this time at all. But those five on the end were the ones what done it last time!"

***

I flagged a guy over in radar one day who was flying low in a posted fifty kph zone.

When I got to his car door he rolled the window down and said, "Please forgive me officer. My wife just called me at the office and is very upset."

"What seems to be the problem?" I asked with concern.

"She was in tears," he said. "She got a speeding ticket this morning and I was rushing home to be at her side."

***

I was having a particularly good day when I stopped a guy for speeding. He looked out the window and gave me the old line, "Don't you have anything better to do than write me a ticket?"

Obliging officer that I was, I said, "Just a moment, sir, I'll check." I pulled out my portable radio and called, "2816 to dispatch."

"Go ahead, 2816."

"I have a driver stopped here who wants to know if I have anything better to do than write him a speeding ticket. Do you have any calls waiting for me?"

"Standby 2816 ... no I don't. You go right ahead and write that ticket."

"Sorry, sir, guess I'll have to see your license."

***

I was concerned one time over a vehicle that was travelling in the radar beam at varying speeds. As I watched the readout it waffled from sixty to eighty and then down to thirty and back up to sixty-five. When I pulled the elderly lady over I asked her if she was having car trouble.

"Not at all, young man," she replied indignantly. "Mopsy, my poodle, likes to ride in my lap, and I just can't see over her. When I lean forward to look I push down on the gas pedal. It happens all the time!"

***

Traffic cops find themselves the target of many a person's ill feelings for having been stopped. Every now and then a response to a summons produces some worthwhile reading such as the following which was received after a summons was issued:

To Whom It May Concern,

I did not:
1) Run a red light
2) Run over a pedestrian
3) Drive the wrong way on a oneway street
4) Drive while impaired
5) Have drugs in the trunk of my car
6) Beat my child
7) Steal anything
8) Rape
9) Pillage
10) Plunder
11) Exceed the speed limit
12) Disobey playground zone signs
13) Litter
14) Set fire to a building
15) Neglect to pay taxes
16) Neglect to pay bills
17) Murder
18) Stab someone

However, I did turn right between 7:00 and 9:00 A.M. when I wasn't supposed to. When I apologized the cop said it wasn't the end of the world. "My question is, if it wasn't the end of the world, then why do I have to pay this ticket?"

***

A sergeant was on stakeout around Christmas time. He'd been watching a place for two nights and it was bitterly cold. He didn't like to leave the car running because he was nervous about carbon monoxide, so he decided to bring an electric heater with him. When he got to the stakeout he backed his car up beside a house and ran an extension cord from the heater to the Christmas tree on the front lawn. It worked like a charm and he was nice and warm in the car. He'd been there for a while when he saw his suspect down at the end of the street. He started the car, threw it into drive, and gave pursuit. Of course, he forgot to unplug the heater and he stripped that Christmas tree of lights in a flash. The tree bent to the ground and when the lights let go it catapulted snow clear over the roof into the back yard. He raced off after the guy with about one hundred and fifty Christmas bulbs following him down the road.

***

I used to work in one of the more wealthy areas of town. A lot of people I stopped for tickets would give me the standard lines like,

"I'll have your job! You can't give me that ticket, I have contacts!" A day never went by that I didn't hear it from someone.

I stopped a lady and took her driver's license back to the police car to write the ticket. I noticed there was a condition code which said she had to wear corrective lenses in order to drive.

When I had stopped her I hadn't seen any glasses, so I stomped back to her car and asked brusquely, "Where are your glasses?"

The lady looked at me and replied in the same tone as my question, "I have contacts!"

I bent down to her window and stated, matter-of-factly, "I don't care who you know, you're getting this ticket anyway!"

She leaned out the window and pointed to her eyes. "I don't wear glasses, you Ditz! I have contact lenses!"

"I knew that!" I said, passing her the ticket and beating a humble retreat.

***

There's an area of Calgary famous for its gay population. The residents of the area complained about the prostitution there and the traffic it caused at three o'clock in the morning.

I was filling in a check-up slip on anything that moved, and after a few weeks we got to know the regulars. We had dealt with one particular guy quite a few times during the operation and when he saw us he wasn't afraid to talk. The pressure made the prosties move for a while and the assignment was terminated.

A few months later I was in the area again on a call, and I saw the same guy outside one of the bars.

We pulled up and I said, "Hi guy. How's things goin'?"

He came over to the car and started talking just as a loud vehicle went by.

He said, "Oh, jutht living with a trick, it'th a real drag!"

I leaned out the window and said, "Living with a chick, hey, that's a step in the right direction."

He scowled at me, "Oh God no, not a chick ... a trick. Get it right thtupid!"

***

Noisy parties can be fun to deal with. I remember getting sent to one in some condos. They were designed so that you went through the door and up a long set of stairs to get to the living room. Before we drove onto the block we could hear the stereo. This was a loud one!

I got out of the car and started knocking on the door. No one came. I hammered real hard, but nobody answered. I waited until the songs were changing and I kicked the door as hard as I could. Still they refused to answer. I was going to call the sergeant to get permission to kick it in when I tried the knob. It was unlocked.

As we started up the stairs, I hollered, "What's the matter? Are all of you deaf in here?"

I was upset by the time I got to the top of the stairs. I was just about to yell again when I saw everybody sitting around a table and flapping their hands ... in sign language.

***

It was my second night on the street and we were chasing a guy with a gun in his car. He said he wanted to kill a policeman. He lost it on a corner and slammed hard into a power pole. The guys in the police car ahead of us jumped out to affect the arrest, and I bailed out of the driver's seat, adrenalin pumping. I knew this guy had a gun in the car and I was sure I was the policeman he wanted to kill.

As I got out of the car I drew my weapon.

It caught on the retracting seatbelt and flipped out of my hand. I grabbed for it three times before it deep-sixed in a mud puddle. I lost my balance and ran through the puddle, creating giant waves and a tremendous ruckus.

My officer coach turned to me, shaking his head, and asked, "Are you finished?" When the other guys came back with the bad guy under arrest, there I was on my hands and knees in the water fishing for my gun.

***

Somebody saw a suitcase beside one of the police cars in the locked compound downtown. It looked out of place so the fellow called it into the E-line. One of our zone cars was sent to check it out, and when they saw it they were sure it was a bomb. The compound was locked, and the case was stuffed in between two marked police cars.

I was sent to the perimeter and told to stop traffic in the area. The bomb squad was notified and came down with their steel tank and all the fancy stuff they use.

After examination, they decided that it was a bomb and would have to destroy it. They used their new robot to put the thing into the blast canister. We had traffic snarled for hours all the way out of the city to the detonation site.

The press was there taking pictures from a safe distance, and even the police video unit was there to record the event for training purposes. We all watched as they wired the case and then retreated behind a shield. The explosion was a sight to see. The suitcase and contents were blown into pieces smaller than nickels. What a rush!! Just as the last of the debris was floating gently down, the dispatcher came over the air.

"Mr. Smith was arrested on warrants at the airport last night and has been released. His suitcase with all of his belongings has gone missing from the police compound where it was left by mistake. Anyone knowing anything about it please contact the headquarters duty inspector immediately."

***

Impaired driving detail always gives you lots of stories to tell. I stopped a truck in a back alley. We had the driver out and were dealing with him in the back seat of the police car. I looked across the lawn to the house in front of us, and I saw a woman stagger out onto the grass. She looked blitzed. She groped around and finally made it to the fender of the truck where she grabbed it like there was no tomorrow.

I leaned out the window and hollered,

"Hey, come here."

She stopped a second, and then crawled around the fender of the truck and tried to get into it. She didn't seem to be responding very well.

I yelled again, "Hey, come here!"

She stopped again for a second, and then went right back to what she was doing. I don't like being ignored, so I leaned out of the window and bellowed at her, "Hey, what's the matter with you? Are you blind? I said come here!"

She fell out of the truck and staggered to the fender of the police car.

When she got to the window she looked right past me and said soberly, "Yes, I am. What did you want?"

***

When I was in K-9 we had to do what was called a bonding walk with our dogs. This was a quiet time with your dog so he got to like you and didn't bite you when you were at a call. The walk was about ten miles, and near the end I was getting a little played out. I decided to take a short-cut and came to a ten-foot-tall chain link fence.

We had learned to do fences with the dogs and I had him over in a flash. As I was climbing over myself I noticed about fifteen or

so nurses standing on a balcony at the hospital across the tracks. I had my TAC suit on so I had to be real cool. When I got up onto the fence I saw that the pipe holding it was broken, and the section was really unsteady. As I swung my leg over the mesh buckled. I toppled forward with a great grunt, and my boot got caught in the top of the links. There I was, hanging upside down by one leg.

The dog started jumping up and down, licking my face, and thinking, "Oh, what a good game."

About this time the nurses started clapping. To top things off it was morning rush hour on the main drag and traffic was bumper-to-bumper, stop and go. All these people were looking at me wondering what in hell this policeman was doing hanging upside down on a fence.

CHAPTER THREE

Well, how are we doing so far? Have we managed to maintain a professional status at all times? Are we securing the macho image of the highly trained professional? NOT! As you can surely see by now policemen are human. They suffer the same foibles and quirks as everyone else, and no branch of the service escapes the silly bug. When the stupid bug bites you find yourself helplessly infected. No one is immune to the nasty little critter.

Policemen feed on humour like sharks in a feeding frenzy or wolves at a kill ... a flurry of flashing white teeth, a streak of raking claws, the curl of the attacker's lip twisted in determination. When the action subsides and the blue wall fades from the scene, all that remains is the tattered and battered distinctive box from Tim Hortons. A regular diet of doughnuts and humour serves as a relief valve for tension and stresses applied in generous helpings to the police officer on a daily basis.

Bank robberies are not funny, especially to the staff on the receiving end of the bad guy's demands. However, even the criminal is unable to escape the bite of the silly bug. How about the robber who presented a hold-up note to the teller, grabbed the money and fled ... leaving the note behind ... written on the back of one of his own personalized cheques. Or the bank robber who had an unsuspecting taxi waiting for him in the fire lane at the front of the bank. When he fled with the loot he couldn't get the back door of the taxi open, so he started kicking it and screaming at the driver to let him in. The driver was only too obliged to do so as he was a police officer in an unmarked car who was writing a ticket to the taxi driver for stopping in the fire lane.

Then there was the would-be gunman who stormed into the bank lobby and announced his intention to relieve the establishment of its finances. When people turned to look at him he realized he had forgotten to pull down his mask. In one deft, or daft, movement he swung a pillowcase over his head, and with a determined snap pulled it to his shoulders. It would have been to his benefit to have pre-cut the eye-holes because while he was completely blinded in the pillowcase the customers attacked him, disarmed him and kept him "in the dark," so to speak, until police arrived.

Humour can also be an effective tool in the solving of crimes if it is properly and sensitively applied. For example, an officer should not attend at a domestic dispute and drop a few Rodney Dangerfield lines like, "Take my wife --- please!" I would think such an officer might find himself quickly in search of gainful employment elsewhere. On the other hand, humour can be used as a tension breaker to gain valuable information.

A constable attended a bank robbery in which the culprit had fired a shot. Everyone at the bank was understandably shaken. Any robbery investigator will tell you that when a gun has been pointed and/or fired during the commission of an offence, the descriptions vary wildly. One witness will say he was six foot five inches, another five foot seven inches, he had a beard, he was cleanshaven, the gun was four feet long, it was a huge handgun, black, silver, rifle, pistol ... a nightmare. This particular officer was getting nowhere fast --- about as fast as the bad guy was getting away.

He finally called out in a loud voice, "I used to be a teacher. I'll be grading your reports for content, grammar, and spelling!"

Now, we wouldn't suggest the constable quit his day job to become a stand up comic. As a matter of fact we would recommend that he does not, but his one-liner served the purpose and as a result a complete, accurate description was obtained that resulted in the subsequent arrest of the offender.

My favourite bank robber of all times was the culprit who stomped into the bank and yelled at the top of his lungs, "Put your stickin' hands in the air, this is a fuck-up!" Read on please ...

***

I am a firm believer that every police-man on the street should present as spit and polished from head to toe. I like to see creases that you could cut yourself on in the pant legs, and I take great pride in my dress and deport-ment. One cold winter day there were no cars left to use. So I went to the police garage and they gave me the keys to a spare car parked in the roof storage area. Up I went to find that the car hadn't been used in months, and it was filthy.

I decided to run it through the car wash before daring to drive it on the street. Down the parkade ramp I drove with dust flying from the car at every corner. I pulled up to the wash bay and the doors slid open. Already I could imagine the dust and dirt flowing down the drain. I pulled into the bay and the doors fell gently behind me.

A ripple of excitement coursed through my veins as the spray commenced and the whirling brushes began stroking the outside of the car. I watched with anticipation as the brushes moved along the body of the vehicle, stripping it clean and shining the metallic surface below. Round and round they went half way along the body and then abruptly stopped, though still rotating. The spray cascaded over the hood, but the brushes refused to move.

I had two choices. I could call on the radio for the garage mechanic to come out and fix this thing for one. I don't think so! I would be the laughing stock of the shift.

My other choice was to back the car up as far as I could inside the wash bay, open the door, and dart past the deluge to the emergency exit at the side. I decided this was the least risky method. No one would be aware of my ridiculous predicament.

Having backed the car up, I took a deep breath and flung the door open. In a flash I was rushing past the spray nozzles without a drop on my neatly pressed uniform. God, I was good! I reached the exit door and as I grabbed for it I stepped on the only piece of ice on the wash bay floor. Down I went, spiraling along the cement like a curling rock. I slid right into the brushes, which by now were

70

beginning to wear the paint off the sides of the car. The tire brushes licked my glasses like a lonely puppy.

When I was finally able to extricate myself I sloshed out of the bay, covered from head to foot in suds like a homemade ad for Tide.

***

I was assigned to the Traffic Investigation Section which handles fatal motor vehicle accidents. I was at a particularly extensive accident scene one night with car parts and skid marks all over the place. We decided to enlist the aid of our accident reconstructionist to assist us in detailing the scene on paper. He is the highly trained specialist who has studied crash dynamics and physics and knows all about accidents. There were dozens of pieces strewn about the roadway and liquid spills running in every direction. When the reconstructionist arrived he took a brief look at the chaotic scene and began explaining to us what, in his opinion, had taken place.

About half way through his explanation he stopped and looked at a trail of liquid that was out of place. It didn't seem to fit with the rest of the damage or placement of the vehicles.

"It doesn't look like anti-freeze," he said as he stood over the trail. "And it sure as hell isn't battery acid. What the blazes is it?"

He reached down and stuck his finger into the trickle. With a quick flip he brushed his fingertip across his tongue. Just as he was doing so, a constable stepped out of the bushes zipping up his fly.

"I'm sorry," he said, "I just couldn't hold it any longer ..."

***

A long, long time ago we used to drive Rambler Ambassadors for police cars. The front seat leaned too far forward. My partner and I used to spend the shift putting our feet on the dashboard and trying to push the seat upright. We had worked at it for some weeks now and nearly had the problem rectified.

We stopped at a traffic light, and when it turned green we were off like a flash. We heard a thunderous crack, and as we looked at each other wide-eyed the seat brackets gave way. Our knees came up, our heads flew backwards, and we both tumbled unceremoniously into the rear passenger compartment. I was barely able to hold onto the steering wheel with my fingertips as we fled the traffic lights, tires smoking and brake pedal just out of reach.

I groped for the wheel as I saw my partner's ass fly past my face and disappear.

"Holy shit!" he yelled as he landed amid the coats, hats and briefcases in the rear of the car.

When I finally got the damn thing stopped a citizen pulled alongside and slowed. He looked at my partner's feet pressed against the rear window and my enlarged eyes peeking at him over the door lock. He smirked, chuckled, then screamed with laughter and drove away.

**

There was a particular sergeant in one area whom no one cared for. This man went out of his way to make things miserable for everyone and appeared to enjoy the process. His one vice was that he loved to smoke a pipe. He used to sit in the office and puff on that thing, rocking back and forth in his chair.

One night he left the office to do something and forgot his pipe on the desk. I had just made a drug bust and had seized a bag of marijuana which was destined for the property room. On the way past his office I quietly slid in and dumped the pipe. In seconds I had it full to the brim with M.J., and a few of us stood around the corner to watch.

The sergeant returned shortly and lit his pipe. He began rocking and puffing, and rocking and puffing and smiling and grinning and laughing. Pretty soon the smoke was so thick you could cut it with a knife. When we peaked around the corner he had this beautiful glow on his face. That was the best shift we ever had with him.

***

I had a warrant to arrest a fellow in a seedier area of town. At the door we were invited in by a very large man with muscles on his muscles.

His first statement after we placed him under arrest was, "Do you think you could take me if I decided not to go?"

"Well," I said, "probably not. But we'll have to try and undoubtedly we'll make an awful mess of your house in the attempt!"

At this point, the man's wife convinced him to leave peaceably with us. A wise decision we thought! Once in the police car I began talking to Mr. Muscle who was in the rear seat. As I spoke to him I turned half way around in the front seat and sat with my arm over the top of the bench. Suddenly, the man grabbed my arm with both of his huge hands, and bent it downward over the back of the seat with just enough pressure to hurt a little.

"Let me give you some advice, young man," he said with a grin. "When you have a prisoner in the back seat, never, never put your arm up here. I could twist it down like this and break it!"

My free hand flashed down and snapped my .38 revolver out of its holster. I quickly jammed the barrel into his left nostril.

"Let me give you some advice," I said. "Never, never try to break someone's arm when that person has a gun up your nose!"

He let go of my arm and sat back. "Good point, good point," he said.

***

Some years ago I was at an accident scene in which a vehicle with two persons in it had driven into the rear of a semi-trailer. Ambulance personnel declared the men dead and after extricating the first body from the wreckage, one of the paramedics came to speak with me. He said they would take the first body to the morgue and then come back for the other, rather than call out another ambulance. Away they went.

My partner and I continued with the investigation of the scene and had to gather some information from the car. He leaned

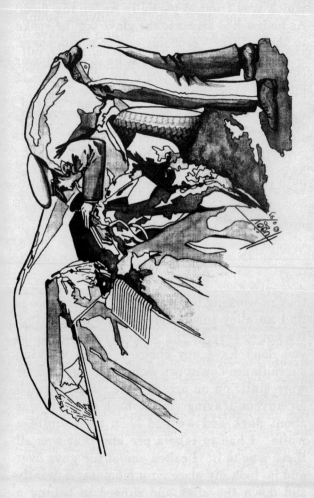

into the window and reached around the body which was trapped partially under the dash. As he reached across to the glove box, he spoke to the cadaver - probably out of nervousness.

"Excuse me," he said as he stretched over the limp form, "How you doin' in there, good buddy?"

"Oooh ... not ... bad ..." came the answer. "When are you going to get me outta here?"

"You're alive!" my partner yelled.

"I better be," replied the man, "or we're both in trouble. You talk to dead guys often?"

***

It's easy for men to have a pee when they're working because all they have to do is find an alley somewhere and do their thing. It's not so easy for the women, but sometimes you don't have any choice. I was working surveillance downtown some time ago and we were static on an arcade. We were to watch for anyone leaving via the back door. It was about dusk and we had been there quite a while. I had to take a pee and that was all there was to it! I called one of the guys over and he took my place for a moment. I quietly slid down the alley and slipped in behind a nice dark garbage bin. I dropped my drawers and gave a sigh of relief as I emptied my bladder. No sooner had I begun than a hand reached out and grabbed my ankle from under the bin. I screeched and bolted into the alley trying to pull up my pants. I don't know who got the bigger laugh, my partners or the drunk under the garbage bin!

***

I was impressing my rookie one day with how much I knew about the area to which we were assigned and the bad guys we dealt with. We were dispatched to an intrusion alarm at a school and he didn't know how to get there. I was proudly giving him directions, and he was showing me how quickly he could handle the car in response to my lefts and rights. We turned the corner and sped down a little side street which I knew well and would put us at the school faster. He accelerated hard and confidently with the tiniest self-satisfied smirk on his face. About half way down the street, and going much too quickly to avoid disaster, we noticed a gaping hole left by the city crew. With a screeching of brakes and vocal chords we careened into the pit with a solid slam. The car rocked for a brief moment, settled into the hole, and then with a death gasp, broke in two. Believe me, there is no way on this earth to tow a vehicle in two pieces without the public and the other car crews seeing it!

***

Sometimes a practical joke is just too good to be passed up. We played one on a rookie and even managed to get some of the brass involved. Someone decided that this rookie should be given a pair of "test socks" to wear and gather public opinion as to their suitability to the uniform. The socks were the brightest neon red we could find. We enlisted the help of the Quartermasters sergeant and our local staff sergeant.

The rookie was presented with the socks and a memo from the staff sergeant instructing him to wear them and show them to the public. He was to make note of their responses and submit them in report form. I have never seen so many uncomfortable people in my life. How do you tell a policeman that you don't like his socks? Better still, how do you refrain from guttural laughter when he shows them to you? He finally discovered the ruse and took the socks off, but not before the newspapers got hold of the story and printed it. The rookie has since left the job for other reasons, but his memory will live on in the annals of the department as the victim of the "Red Socks Caper."

***

Several years ago we were suffering numerous break-ins at gas stations. The culprits were hiding in the washrooms and then knocking out walls without being seen from the street. I was patrolling an alley on foot one night when I heard the sound of a muffled jack hammer coming from the washroom of a nearby service station. I crept to the door, and as I listened I could hear the drill starting and stopping. I could imagine the bad guy lifting the drill and taking pieces of the concrete wall out as I stood this close to him. Buzzz, clink, clink. Buzzz, clink, clink. I had him trapped and he didn't even know it. There was going to be a commendation in this for me!

Flashlight in one hand and gun in the other, I stepped boldly to the door. In one swift move I kicked the door and stepped in.

"Hold it right there," I yelled into the washroom. "You're under arrest!"

I ducked as I saw him staring back at me holding a gun. Just then the door bounced off the wall and struck me in the arm. At the exact same moment, the faulty air compressor started up again. I came "that close" to blowing away my reflection in the washroom mirror. I decided to close the door and quietly seek my commendation elsewhere.

***

I was just out of classes and was patrolling in the eastern portion of the city. We were sitting at the lights on a main street when an impaired driver came through the intersection and drove straight into the side of our police car. My partner couldn't get out of his door, so I jumped out to arrest the drunken person - my first bust!

I bolted from the car and walked to the driver's door. The old fellow who was at the wheel looked up at me with a liquored grin and said, "Boy, it didn't take you guys long to get here."

***

It was one of those winter days. The roads were coated with ice and we went to accident after accident all day. We were sent to one at the bottom of a very bad hill, and when we arrived we discovered there were six cars involved. I got out of the car and hung onto the fender as I tried to walk to the motorists whose vehicles were crumpled. It was treacherous! I looked over my shoulder and I could see a car beginning to come down the hill. I turned to him and waved him back.

I was amazed as I watched him continue towards me. I started yelling and waving frantically at him, but he kept on coming. About half way down the hill he locked his brakes and started to slide. He skated right into the pile of cars and stopped.

I went over to his door (I must admit I was a little p.o.'d at this guy) and said to him, "Didn't you see me waving my arms?"

"Yeah, I saw you," he said, "but I thought you were waving me down here."

"Listen," I replied, "I was trying to tell you to stay up there cause it's too icy. Now that you're here give me your license and papers. We'll have to add you to the accident report."

He passed me the papers and I closed his door with fervour. I was upset. As I turned to stomp back to the police car my feet came out from under me and I slid on my back right under the guy's car.

He opened the door and called, "Officer, are you all right?"

"No problem," I said, "just checking for undercarriage damage."

***

Patrolling the bar parking lots is a standard on weekend nights and you never know what you'll see. We were driving up and down the rows of parked cars when I yelled out "Stop!" My partner hit the brakes and we both watched a girl, dressed to the nines, standing up from a pee and straightening her dress. When she saw us she became embarrassed but approached the car.

"I'm sorry, officers," she blurted. "I don't usually do this but I had to go so bad. I suppose you want to see my identification."

"Why not," I replied, "we've seen everything else."

***

I worked with a guy who chewed tobacco. After a few shifts he suggested that I try some and tossed me the package. As he did so, a man came up to his window to talk and my partner became engaged in conversation with him. Left to myself, I decided to give this stuff a try. I opened the lid and took a sniff. It smelled pretty good. Not knowing exactly what to do I took a pinch as I had seen my partner do, and popped it into my mouth. With great exuberance I chomped down on the wad. If you have ever experienced chewing tobacco, you, of course, know that you don't chew it, you put it inside your lip and let it sit.

When you do chew it, like I did, your

mouth immediately fills to capacity with saliva which is trying to dilute the tobacco. My mouth was so full it was starting to squirt out between my bulging lips. I had to get rid of this stuff. As I rolled down my window to spit, an elderly lady stepped up to the car to ask directions. By this time, the juice was spurting out and I was cross-eyed. I opened the door and got out, quickly running to the back of the car. The lady, thinking I was ill, came to my rescue. I didn't want to do this in front of her, so I ran around to the driver's side of the car where the man was talking to my partner. The saliva was still coming and my cheeks were ballooned as I desperately looked for a place to spit. The lady was following me as I stumbled past my partner. I looked over at him as I went past and he saw me. Of course he burst into laughter. Now the guy was looking at me too as I ran around the front of the car pursued by the lady. Finally, my cheeks ready to burst, I let forth the tides and spit. By now the lady caught up to me and was patting my back.

"There, there dear," she said. "It always feels better when you get rid of it."

***

I was walking the beat downtown one day near the bus station when I saw a man leaning up against a wall. As I got closer to him I realized that he was intoxicated and his fly was open with his privates hanging out. It was six-thirty in the morning and traffic was beginning to build. People were driving past and viewing this. Young and eager constable that I was, I decided to speak with the man.

I stepped in front of him to block the scene from the public and I said, "Get yourself cleaned up and covered up."

About this time, two of my colleagues came around the corner and walked towards me. I was about to show them how I could take care of this situation when I felt something warm on my leg. I looked down and the guy was relieving himself, right onto my fresh clean pants.

***

Doing a report and laying the charges against a shoplifter is not a major task. In fact, you become so familiar with it that the call becomes routine and usually goes off without a hitch. I was doing just that one day in a mall with two levels. The store where the alleged thief had been captured was on the second level and directly opposite a balcony which overlooked a public seating area on the main floor.

I had completed the paperwork in record

time, given the accused her copy of the court notification, and was leaving the store. I suddenly had a haunting feeling that something had not gone right. I quickly ran through my procedure, but I was sure I had forgotten to do something important. I walked towards the front of the store while checking my clipboard. The report was complete and I was skimming over the court documents as I strolled past the checkout. It was near Christmas and there was a long line-up of customers waiting to pay for their shopping at the cashier.

As I went past the line-up, someone wished me Merry Christmas. I nodded, still engrossed in my papers. The front of the store was open, except for a line of silver posts to prevent people from taking the shopping carts from the premises. Without breaking my stride I steamed directly into one of those posts which caught me right in the scrotum. I instantly doubled over in agony and my hat flew off. By this time I had struck the bottom of the post with my boot, causing a loud clang to ring out. The entire mall turned in my direction. My hat sailed away from me, caught the edge of the balcony railing, and disappeared onto the main level. By now my face was a mixture of red and green. I felt right in season.

CHAPTER FOUR

MURPHY'S LAW: If anything can go wrong ... it will!!

Poor Murphy can't even be properly recognized for the creation of this law. All we know is that it's a twentieth-century axiom, the originator of which is obscure. Murphy, you couldn't get the authorship of your law right either! However, I'm sure that when Murphy discovered and coined his law, he had the police services in mind. On this job when things go wrong it's usually at the most inopportune time. The application of Murphy's Law to our department also proves its potential to be proportionate. Let me explain:

- A police officer's need to stop at a gas station for a pee is directly proportionate to the urgency of the call he has been dispatched to.
- Equipment and uniform inspection will only take place when you have run out of shoe polish and the constable you are standing beside on parade is a rookie who still spit-shines his boots.

- Your craving for a cup of coffe is directly related to the number of highpriority calls waiting in your area.
- The inspector always shows up when you are a few minutes late for pre-shift parade.
- The inspector never shows up when you are early for pre-shift parade.
- The media will arrive at an accident scene and begin taking film footage only when you are out of the police car with out your hat.
- The media will edit out all the unnecessary accident footage except the part where you were standing beside a damaged vehicle scratching your ass.
- The cute waitress with "blue fever" will prefer your partner to you.
- The waitress with "blue fever" who prefers you will not be cute.
- The amount of overtime you have to put in at the end of your shift is directly proportionate to how "hot" the date was that you had arranged for after work.
- A drunk's projectile vomiting will always seek out the constable who has just put on a freshly cleaned uniform that shift.
- The staff sergeant in Communications will never monitor radio transmissions ... until you pick up the mike and say

something incredibly stupid.

- How you dress for work will determine your assignment for the day. If you dress in six layers ready for minus thirty-five degree celsius, you will be assigned to office duties because someone has booked off sick.

- The distance you are from the district office during a torrential rainstorm determines the traffic point to which you will be assigned at an injury accident when you have forgotten your rain gear.

I remember being assigned with my partner one night to watch a car at a certain location and to follow it if it moved. We took the assignment seriously and sat in a parking lot across the street from the vehicle, watching intently. We were in an unmarked police car and the emergency equipment rack, a piece of metal strip about twelve inches long covered with buttons and switches, was installed against the dashboard between the passenger and driver's seats. Two uneventful hours passed before the bad guys showed up at the car. Our position in the parking lot put street light behind us. When the guys arrived we slid down in our seats so as not to be "made." My partner's knee hit the bottom of the switch rack and slid up it with impeccable accuracy. Every piece of emergency equipment we had was activated. The red dashlight came on, the red and blue grill lights came on, the flashing wig-wag headlights came on and to boot, the air horn sounded. Here endeth the great stakeout, thanks to Murphy.

Murphy even controls simple traffic stops. A not very courteous driver cut me off one day and sped away. I was in an unmarked car so I took up the task and paced him for speeding as well. When I had a good clock on him I activated the emergency lights and pulled him over. I was a little upset at his having cut me off and when I unfastened my seatbelt, I tossed it with fervour over my shoulder. The plastic cover had long since been broken off the belt and there was a little square hole in the centre for fastening the buckle to the clasp. As Murphy would have it, the little square hole dropped neatly over the round lock knob on my door. Twist, pull, and turn as I did, it would not come off. There I sat, trapped in my own car.

After a few moments the driver got out of his van and came back to see what I wanted. As he approached I rolled down my window and put my arm out, covering the door lock.

"Did you want to see me?" he asked.

"Yes," I said in my best professional voice. "You were driving a little fast ... but I'm just giving warnings today. Please slow down."

Ah, Murphy, what would we do without you?

"DON'T SWEAT IT ... THIS UNIFORM IS ONLY
A POLICY CHANGE ...
IT'LL CHANGE AGAIN NEXT WEEK!"

Riding a police motorcycle is exhilarating to say the least. Picture yourself perched on a shiny blue and white Harley, the envy of John Q. Public. Spit and polished, you present an impressive spectacle to all. I was on a main street one beautiful summer day cruising along at less than the speed limit, to enjoy the lunch time ladies as they walked and talked. I noticed a black Camaro following me so I slowed a little to let it catch up and grab a peek inside. When the car pulled next to me I felt like I was in American Graffiti. She was beautiful, blonde, and smiling at me.

I took up pace with her and we drove side by side for about a block, smiling back and forth, not saying a word. We came to a red light and she stopped at the corner. I pulled alongside, grinning my biggest grin. I was so enthralled by her I forgot to put my foot down, and while I was smiling away my Harley fell over onto the sidewalk, trapping me underneath. The light turned green and that was the last I saw of her, thank God!

***

It was a hot, hot July day, and I was doing radar duty on a well-travelled but as yet unimproved roadway. The only place to park was on the side of the road partially in a ditch, and there I was, writing away. Each time I stepped from the car I thought I could smell smoke but I wasn't sure. I looked around but couldn't see anything on fire. The horizon was clear, though the smell of smoke drifted near every now and then. Soon I heard sirens and now really wondered what was burning. I was in the car with my head down writing my notes on the back of a summons when a fire truck pulled in behind me and stopped. One of the firemen came to my car and I looked up at him casually.

"Hi," I said. "Where's the fire?"

"Under your car," he replied, rolling his eyes and shaking his head. "Hot exhaust pipes you know!"

"Shit!" I yelled, bursting from the police car and running a few feet away. "My sergeant was right, this is a hot place to run radar!"

***

Death is not funny, but it has its moments. I was dispatched to a call where a rather large young man had passed away in his sleep. After confirming it was a natural death, the Medical Examiner released the body for transport to the morgue. I had to help move the fellow as he was too large for one to lift, and the body removal guy was by himself. My sergeant also attended at the residence and was in the living room with the family doing his professional best to console them. We had to take the stretcher down a hall and then make a ninety degree turn to exit via the front door. This guy was really tall and we had to stand him up to turn the corner. The family was all quiet and the sergeant was trying to distract them as we fumbled with the stretcher. We finally made the turn. Just as we were moving quietly past the living room, the sergeant's electric wristwatch alarm went off ... playing "Roll Out the Barrel". We dashed for the door and managed to hold ourselves together until the watch, still chiming away, sailed over our heads onto the lawn.

***

Many a cop is guilty of taking a whiz in a back alley on night shift. Sometimes you just can't make it to a bathroom. I was in K-9 and had been patrolling the industrial area for a few hours. I had to pee so bad I knew I wasn't going to make it much further. I pulled into a dark alley and stepped up against a door where I immediately began to relieve myself. Suddenly the door burst open and a guy ran out with a bag of loot from the office. He ran right into my arms.

With penis in hand I yelled at him, "Police, you're under arrest ... soon as I finish here!"

He didn't dare ask.

***

A certain inspector got onto a health kick and started to go to a public pool every noon hour for a swim. His secretary went to his gym bag one day and removed his bathing trunks. She replaced them with a pair of black lace panties and bra. The inspector headed off to the pool in uniform and went to the locker room with all the guys to change. He opened the bag and flipped out his towel to sit on. Flutter, flutter, flutter went the bra and panties onto the floor.

"How long have you been wearing those?" one of the sergeants asked him with a wry smile.

Not missing a beat, the inspector replied, "Ever since my wife found them in the glove box of my car."

***

Two off-duty constables were on their way home from a movie one night when they saw an impaired driver whose driving could not be ignored. He had a flat tire and had driven the rubber right off the rim. This guy was so bad he had to be stopped. They followed him for a while trying to figure out how to get him to pull over when he drove off the road and jumped out of the car. He started to run across a field and the two constables raced after him. Even though he was drunk he was making good time, and it was evident that the foot chase had a good chance of being prolonged.

One of the constables yelled, "City Police, stop or I'll let the dog go!"

The other constable, being as witty as the first, started barking, "Woof, woof, woof!" The guy stopped and put his hands up. You should have seen him looking around for the dog all the way back to the car.

***

I was involved in a chase one night and the offender was absolutely crazy. He drove everywhere that car would go and a few places it wouldn't. I finally got him boxed in in traffic and I put the police car tight against his rear bumper. I jumped out of the car and took my night stick with me expecting a fight. As I got to his door he locked it, so I drew back with the stick to break the window. I drove the stick at the window with tremendous force, and to my astonishment, the butt end carried through into the car, unrestricted, and I struck the guy square in the left ear. The crazy bugger had his window rolled down. I thought I'd killed him!

***

We spotted four guys in a stolen car. They led us on a short chase and we finally got them stopped on a side street. Just as we pulled up, all four doors flew open and they tried to get out. In order to avoid a foot chase, I pulled up tight to the car and gave it a short tap with the push bumpers. The four of them fell back into their seats and we had them contained quickly.

As I took the driver out and was cuffinghim, he looked at me and said, "What the fuck's the matter with you? Don't you know how to drive?"

***

I took my rookie partner to an alarm in a residential area.

As soon as we arrived he baled out of the car and ran up the driveway yelling at me, "I'll cover the back!"

He raced around the corner, scaled a six foot board fence, and in a single leap fell face-first into the swimming pool.

***

I had a ride-along with me one winter day and a rookie partner as well. The girl was a police science student and wanted to see first-hand what police work was really like. First stop - the police carwash. As we were leaving, the fog rolled out of the wash bay ahead of me, and I couldn't see a thing. About half way out the door came down and caught the light rack on the top of the car. The bottom edge of the door ripped the light rack right off and bent it back over the rear window.

I stopped, looked at the girl in the back seat, her eyes the size of saucers, and asked, "Well, how do you like police work so far?"

***

I was with a bunch of Bobbies in a pub one night while on vacation in England, and they were showing me a good time. One of the fellows with us had a very good command of the Queen's English and used it as we would normal conversation. There was a man and woman at the next table who obviously had had a few drinks too many.

A couple of local theatre personalities came in and joined us at our table, at which time our well-spoken friend stood up, and in a loud voice announced, "You're a bloody thespian aren't you?"

With that the guy from the next table stood up and smacked him right in the mouth.

Our guy asked, "What the 'ell did you do that for?"

The fellow looked him square in the eye and said, "Cause you said me ladyfriend 'ere was a lesbian!"

***

I was sitting at the traffic lights, minding my own business, waiting for the green. Just as the light changed a black Mustang

T.A.C. TEAM ON A DAY OFF

went roaring past me at a pretty good clip. I turned on the overhead lights and tramped the accelerator to the floor. This guy was not going to get away from me! I was in full acceleration and rapidly catching up to him. Just as I tapped the siren button he hit the brakes hard and slowed quickly for me. I stomped on the brake but I was still accelerating. The damn gas pedal stuck to the floor. I sailed right on by the guy looking over my shoulder at him, my eyes like two huge white saucers. He shrugged his shoulders, turned right and disappeared.

***

A long time ago we used to drive Plymouth Satellites for police cars. One night we decided to take our car on a highway run to blow the carbon out and we ended up in Banff, which is a town about one and a half hours west of Calgary. After a short tour and coffee we headed back to the city. We were surprised to hear the dispatcher contacting the cars one by one in an attempt to determine which vehicle had been stolen and was headed for Banff. We decided right there that we had better take the extra mileage off the car some-how, before it was discovered and we had some heavy explaining to do.

Off we went to the nearest dark city park and jacked the back of the car up. Into reverse it went and we waited. The vibrations soon made the jack fall over so we had to find something else to do. We backed the car into a snow drift and let it run. This worked until the tires melted through the ice and started to smoke. We just weren't making any progress.

Then my partner had a brilliant idea. We drove the rest of the shift backwards. Whenever a car went past we slowed down and used the spotlight like we were trying to find an address. By the end of the shift we had taken seventy miles off the odometer.

**

I arrested an impaired driver one night who was pretty mouthy. He wanted to fight, and it lasted about three seconds until he was on the ground in cuffs. We went down in clay powder and were covered from head to toe. You can imagine what we looked like. This fellow was not happy, and all the way back to the car he kept saying, "You guys'll pay for this."

He was right. He crapped himself and we drove all the way downtown with our heads hanging out the window, gagging.

I was in plain clothes detail and we had information that a guy we wanted was staying at a motel nearby. Over we went and knocked on the door, expecting him or his girlfriend to answer. Instead the door was opened by an elderly woman with long grey hair. We were trying to get some information from her when a huge Persian cat appeared from inside the room. It started purring and rubbed against my partner's legs. He gave it a slight push with his ankle and the cat got the message. It came right over to my legs and started the same thing. I gave it a polite shove but it refused to pay attention.

Instead of leaving, it grabbed onto my leg and hung on. I was trying to be nonchalant because we thought the guy we were looking for was in the room. I lifted my leg and gave the cat a shake, but it just grabbed on tighter. Not bad enough, the cat decided that I was fair game and started humping my boot. Now I was really embarrassed. Try as I did, I couldn't shake the damn thing loose. I must have looked like Inspector Clueseau, holding onto the door frame with one hand and violently shaking this humping cat behind me, while trying to seriously interview the lady at the door.

Late one cold winter night a young fellow went speeding past our police car. We gave chase and got him stopped within a block or so. We put him in the back of the patrol car and wrote him out a summons for speeding. On the back in the officer's notes section is a place for a description of the suspect. I was filling this in and asking him the appropriate questions, height, weight, colour of hair and colour of eyes.

When I asked him "Colour of your eyes," he didn't answer.

I asked again. Still no response. I wondered what the blazes was so difficult about his eye colour, and I asked him a third time rather loudly.

This time he replied, "I am."

I turned around to see him sitting there with his hands over his eyes.

"What are you doing?" I asked.

He said, "Covering my eyes like you said."

"No, no. I asked you the colour of your eyes. Why on earth did you think I would tell you to cover your eyes?"

"Well, I thought you were writing something top secret and you didn't want me to see it."

***

I was interviewing a husband at a domestic dispute one night during which the wife had been struck on the face with something. We were attempting to get sufficient information to lay a charge. She didn't want to talk to us, so we decided to see if we could find out from hubby what he had hit her with. He was not about to implicate himself in any way, but said he was willing to give us a statement.

This is what he wrote, "I was standing in the kitchen when a bag of ice went over my shoulder and hit my wife in the face."

***

Nobody likes to meet a radar cop, but I'll bet a few would like to hide and watch some of the antics that go on. I was on radar duty one day with my partner and we had set up in a high offence area. It was a beautiful winter day and we were enjoying the sunshine when a car entered the radar beam at a good rate of speed. I grabbed my summons book and pulled on the door handle. At the same time I hit the door with my shoulder to open it. The damn thing was locked and the car sped by us.

"Okay," I said, "I'll get the next one."

I unlocked the door and tested it. Now I was ready. Soon another speeding car came past and I flung open the door, throwing myself out of the car. To my chagrin, I still had my seatbelt on and I nearly hung myself in it as the second car went past. My partner was by now in uncontrollable fits of laughter, but I remained undaunted. I quietly unsnapped my seatbelt and relaxed back into the car waiting for the next speeding vehicle. As has a habit of happening, another car came by soon, also exceeding the speed limit.

"He's mine!" I yelled, throwing the door open and bolting from the car.

As I stepped out I was putting my hat on, which I had in my right hand. When my foot hit the ground it went into an ice ridge that had been made by the snow plough, and broke through into the freezing water under it. I left the car with such force that I did a complete pirouette with my hat in my hand. The motorist slowed, waved back at me and drove on. "Let's just go for a damned coffee," I said to my screaming partner, tossing my hat and summons folder into the rear seat.

***

No policeman enjoys going to a sudden death call. The atmosphere is understandably one of grieving and pain. Such a call was dispatched to my partner and me and we attended the residence. When we arrived we rang the bell and noticed there were a bunch of newborn kittens in the porch. A mother and daughter answered the door and were quite busy playing with the kittens. They didn't appear too concerned about the happenings. We were rather upset that this poor old fellow was dead in his bed and the family didn't appear to care at all.

In we went and they showed us into the kitchen. As we walked past the bedroom we saw the old fellow lying in bed, flat on his back, mouth wide open. The woman offered us a coffee so we accepted, and she put the cups on the kitchen table which was like an L-shaped breakfast nook. There was a pile of beer bottles and ashtrays on the table, and a fellow sitting in the corner of the nook, passed out, obviously from a party earlier in the night. My partner squeezed in and pushed up against the guy to give me enough room to sit down, and I slid in beside him.

John took his notebook out and was taking down the required information for our report. He was asking questions regarding the date of birth, occupation, etc., of the old fellow. About this time the woman began to look a bit confused, but nonetheless continued to give the information.

The question finally came up, "When

was the last time you saw your father alive?"

"About five minutes ago," she replied.

My partner said, "No, that's not possible, he's dead and has been for more than five minutes since we've been here."

"No, he's not," she said.

With that my partner closed his book and asked, "Well, if your father's not dead, then who is?"

She just pointed to the guy in the corner of the breakfast nook snuggled up to my partner. I thought he was going to crap his drawers before he got out of there.

***

I was on the force in Scotland and was given traffic duty one day. It was a great summer day and I took my tunic off to work in short sleeves. I knew I was going to be at the traffic point for quite some time, so I went to the bathroom beforehand. Out I went to the intersection and was standing there, proud as can be, waving my arms and smiling at all the nice motorists. After a lengthy period, a car pulled up close to me and the driver leaned out.

He said, "Excuse me, constable, but check your fly," then drove off.

I looked down, and not only was my fly open, but there was a piece of bright white shirttail about five inches long standing straight out.

***

A carload of people were stopped for a drug arrest and we had a bunch of bodies in the vehicle. We cuffed the men and searched them on the spot, but there was a rather large-breasted blonde in the front seat whom we suspected was carrying the drugs in her bra or panties. We cuffed her and took all of them into the office for a complete search. As we put the blonde into an interview room, we asked for her name and address in order to check her out for warrants. The answer came in a definite booming male voice.

"Hold it!" I said. "We have a male here. Okay, fella, strip, we're looking for drugs." He obliged and unzipped the back of his dress. When he dropped it and turned around, we were looking at a real pair a ladies breasts.

"Hold it!" I said. "We have a female here. Cover up and someone will be in to see you in a few minutes."

We left the room and called for a police woman to come in and complete the search. In she came and went into the room for the search.

She got down to the lace panties and we heard her yell from inside, "Hold it!"

She stepped out with a red face and said, "We have a male in here."

We decided to let the policewoman search the top half and we searched the bottom half. It was the booking office who had the real fun in deciding where to put him/her.

***

This is a driver's statement from an accident (unedited): "I drive, I turn, I hurt the wall, I sorry."

***

Some witnesses are really helpful in their statements to police. Some are a little ambiguous, like this one who witnessed an assault: "I saw one person dark chasing one person light."

***

I was investigating a fraud one day when a salesperson turned over to me a few copies of credit card slips that had been presented to her by the bad guy. Three of the four had been honoured for purchase, and it was only the fourth which aroused suspicion. The credit card had been stolen from a company named Eagle Elevators, and the bad guy had signed all four slips "Mr. E. Elevator".

***

I got a call of a suspicious person one night and was right in the area. I responded and was on scene in about one minute. When I got there I saw a young teen leaning up against the rear fender of a car, so I jumped out and grabbed him. As I pulled him away from the fender, I saw that he had his fly down and was urinating into the gas tank.

With wide eyes I asked him, "What the hell are you up to?"

He replied, "I'm this guy's paper boy and he hasn't paid his bill for three months."

Moral of the story - Don't piss off your paper boy.

CHAPTER FIVE

Ah, the paper boy. I admire the tenacity of such stout-hearted young people who labour diligently during the wee hours of the morning to bring us the daily news. The truth be known, that's how most policemen find out what's going on in their city - they read it in the paper. So, next time you ask your policeman neighbour what he knows about some current crime, don't let him snow you, he probably read it in the local tabloid.

Paper delivery persons are a brave bunch. They never know what could be awaiting them when they deliver to a policeman's house. Not long ago a rookie, on his day off, was boning up on his shooting techniques. He was practicing what is called dry firing. (The gun is unloaded and one practices drawing and firing at a target, real or imaginary.) The rookie was standing in his front window drawing and dry firing at a picture inside his house when the poor paper boy came to collect. Just as the kid strolled up the walkway the rookie drew, took a shooting stance, and aimed the gun. It was never pointed at the kid, but the angle of vision and the glare on the window made it seem very much so. Off the paper boy ran to a phone and next thing the rookie knew his house was surrounded by police. Lots of experience he got in report writing very quickly!!!

Yet another officer was dry firing at home as he had done on many prior occasions. He always laid the bullets out in front of him on the coffee table, counted them, and then practiced shooting at targets on TV. He had just finished and was starting to reload his weapon when the phone rang. He had inserted one round into the chamber and laid the gun down to answer the phone. Upon his return, he decided to take a few more practice shots. Up came the gun, flip, he closed the cylinder. He pointed it at the TV ... click, click, click ... boooom!! I don't know which was bigger, the hole in the television screen or the poor guy's eyes.

The Firearms Training Section of the Calgary Police Service is very extensive and safety is stressed above all. But, even then, shit happens. I am a marksman within the Service and was asked to come to the firing range one day to assist in the shooting of a file film for a local news station. It wasn't difficult - all I had to do was stand on the firing line and listen for the commands. I simply had to draw and fire at the target until the cameraman had enough footage for his archives.

The instructor was very businesslike and gave his commands in a loud, clear voice. The camera was running and I was ready to perform. On the "load" command I picked up six rounds and promptly dropped them all down range. The instructor stopped the procedure and I went to collect the bullets. I retrieved five of them and then kicked the sixth with my foot. I followed it down range and kicked it again as I tried to pick it up. The round went all the way to the metal backboard and when I returned the cameraman asked, "Isn't it more effective to 'shoot' the bullet???"

Undaunted, I managed to get six rounds loaded into the gun and stood at the ready position. On the next command I drew my weapon and was to fire at the target. For some reason, I still don't know how or why, because it has never happened since, the front sight of my gun caught on something in my holster, and as I drew with lightning reflexes, the gun was yanked from my hand. I threw it with great force down range. So much for my Dirty Harry imitation.

Part of our regular firearm training con

sists of the viewing of a classic video involving a police department from a large western city. A badguy with a handgun was holed up in his get away van and was surrounded by about a dozen police officers. The officers opened fire on the van and dispensed some one hundred rounds or more into the vehicle. Watching the video, I was reminded of the Clint Eastwood movie "The Gauntlet" where dozens of officers were shooting at a bus in which he was hiding. Parts and pieces of the bus were flying in every direction. This was just like it! Glass broke, mirrors shattered, and tires deflated. When the melée subsided a single voice could be heard desperately trying to take command of the situation.

The disembodied voice delivered a classic line, "Come out and you won't get hurt!"

We now carry pepper spray as part of our daily arsenal. Someone in management developed the term for its use as "Temporary Reflexive Inhibition." Obviously the person who coined this terminology had never been sprayed. T.I.R. does not mean Temporary Reflexive Inhibition. Just ask any policeman who has volunteered to be sprayed as part of their training. To them it means Tightly Restricted Intestines because the second thing to slam shut after your eyes is your asshole, believe me!

Well, let's read on as the honour roll of bloopers continues to unfold.

***

This accident statement is word for word and spelling for spelling. The names, of course, have been left out:

"I was draving down 14 street or ave going to get some sigrets from the store and my gerlfrend grabed the stering wheel and yanked it and I lost controll rolled and I was inasint one minat she loves you and anther minat she blames you. Women!"

***

Yet another rather helpful statement from an accident witness:

"There I was standing on the corner when I saw a big black furry thing fly and the traffic stopped."

***

We pulled up behind a car stopped at a yield sign one evening on a back road. We waited patiently, but after a few minutes it became obvious that the car was not about to move. We inched closer for a better look, and discovered that the couple in the car were engrossed in a session of heavy necking and had no idea we were behind them.

My partner picked up the loudhaler and yelled, "Hey lady, the sign says 'yield', not 'submit."

***

When you're taking down a drug house you can't waste time. If the door doesn't open, you open it any way you can. We were at an apartment building one night and the caretaker came up to the unit to let us in. As we stepped off the elevator we heard noises from inside, so the lead man stuck the key into the lock. The caretaker tried to step off the elevator to say something, but he was shoved backwards for his own safety, and also not to spoil the element of surprise. He tried again to speak as the officer twisted the key in the lock to no avail. Finally, we shouldered the door and bolted in. I looked around to see the caretaker with an expression of disgust on his face and his neck caught in the closing elevator door.

He was yelling at us in a semi-strangled voice, "I was just trying to tell you that these are all brand new doors and they stick a little."

"Oops!"

***

Part of a young offender's comeuppance for misbehaving is to write a letter of apology to the victim of their crime. This was forwarded to us from such a case:

"Dear Mom,

I took the car and ran it into a rock. I am sorry. Please don't yell at me cause I already have a headache from the accident."

***

I learned my lesson about practical jokes one day at headquarters. Three detectives were in the change room and I decided to light a firecracker and toss it on top of the lockers above them. I thought it would just stay up there and scare the hell out of them. The lockers were sloped and the thing fell off, exploding amidst the three. I tried to run. They caught me in my office, and two of them held me down while the third guy took out a pair of scissors and cut my tie off right below the knot. Just as they left my phone rang. The voice on the other end said, "Would you come to the chief's office right away? He needs to speak with you."

I thought at first it was part of the set-up, but they hadn't had time to arrange all this. The best I could come up with was to staple my tie back into place and off I went. The chief never did ask me about it, he just looked at me strangely a number of times during the meeting. Once he raised a finger and opened his mouth to speak, then just shook his head and went on with the meeting.

***

Years ago we had an old district office near the boonies which was just a place to have lunch and rattle off a few reports. One night we were headed for the office when we spotted a dead rabbit on the roadside. A good friend of mine was the duty sergeant that night and I had a brainstorm. It was really, really cold and I decided to freeze the rabbit. I put it into a snow drift and bent its legs around to what I thought was about the size of the old round red light on the top of the sergeant's patrol car. In those days their cars were the only ones with red lights, except for the Traffic Division. We used to call them bubble gum machines because that's exactly what they looked like. We left the rabbit for about two hours and then went back. It was very firmly frozen by now. Off we went back to the station, and my partner kept the sergeant busy while I found his car. I forced the rabbit down over the light and then locked his forepaws in position around the bubble. As a last thought, I pulled his ears straight back and then we quietly left.

At about 6:00 A.M. all the sergeants met regularly at a restaurant to have their morning coffee. We made a meet with the other working car crews that night and told them to be near the restaurant at 0600 hours. The sergeant came out of the office (he didn't see the rabbit) and jumped into the car. Away he went to the restaurant for his morning meeting and, of course, at every intersection a police car waited as he drove past. There he went with the rabbit locked onto his red light, ears pointing back like he was doing ninety miles an hour.

At the end of shift we all lined up at headquarters to have roll call. As we were leaving and walking down the alley, a traffic car sped by with light and siren activated, obviously responding to an injury accident. Atop its roof, arms locked around the light and ears pointed straight back, was our friend the rabbit.

***

I stopped a gentleman for speeding at seventy-five in a fifty zone.

I approached him and said, "Excuse me sir, you have been clocked at seventy-five in a fifty zone. Please come to the police car. I will be issuing you a summons."

He retorted, "I couldn't have been going that fast, I just left the intersection back there."

We had some discussion over the point at which I had received the radar reading, and he insisted repeatedly that he had just left the intersection.

I was getting a little flustered at this so I said to him, "I am not going to argue with you, hop into the intersection and have a seat."

He must have understood me because he followed me back to the police car and got in. My partner overheard me and was chuckling as we got in. I started to write the ticket and laid the summons folder against the car horn, at which time I set off the siren and scared the hell out of all of us. My partner was losing it now.

The guy was still arguing with me, so I finally turned to him and said, "You were the only beam in the radar car at the time."

I finished the ticket without opening my mouth further, as it was obviously not func tioning properly that day. After the guy left I figured I needed to change my luck and move to a new spot. This one seemed jinxed.

I drove to a new location and promptly set up. The first car came along and was speeding.

"Aha," I said, "my luck has changed!"

I opened the door, stepped directly into a huge pothole, and fell flat on my face as the car went by. I decided not to run radar any more that day.

***

I was in the Identification Section a while back and was sent with a partner to a house-breaking to gather fingerprint evidence. While we were there, a little girl came into the living room and began showing off her tiny kitten to my partner.

Every few minutes she came up to him and said "Hey, Mister, look at my kitten." My partner, being the kind of guy he was, would stop and pet the kitten and then continue his work. The interruptions continued until it became rather annoying and was interfering with the examination of the residence. To avoid having to pet the kitten again, my partner went to the basement and commenced examining the point of entry. He pulled up a chair and stood on it to dust the windowsill for prints. He found nothing and in one movement turned and jumped off the chair.

At that moment the little girl said, with a somewhat different tone of voice, "Hey Mister, look at my kitten now!"

"WE ALWAYS GET OUR MAN."

It was very flat under his feet. Being the kind of guy he was, my partner went out and bought a new one for her, one that really did have nine lives.

***

As a young detective I worked the drug squad. In those days the guys were a bunch of really different individuals who worked hard and partied hard. We were a very close-knit group. We considered ourselves to be innovative and conducted some totally unique investigations. One of the guys obtained some information which was related to both drugs and a homicide involving two young girls. The bodies had been found just outside the city limits and the forensic lab had never been able to determine a cause of death on them. Information came to us that they had been involved in doing some homemade drugs.

We did some heavy digging and discovered that there was a guy living outside of town in the area of the murders. He had a drug lab on his property and was making MDA. Further intelligence determined that he was a very violent character and that he had built a gun port on each side of his house. He put out the word that if the cops ever showed up there was going to be one hell of a shootout.

One other detective and I were put in charge of laying out a successful plan to take this guy down. It was the middle of February and we decided that the best way to see the lay of the land would be to do a fly-by in a small plane. From the air we might be able to determine if there was anything around the farm house to indicate where the lab might be. We located a police officer who owned an airplane, and he volunteered to help us out. The "craft" was a tiny little thing, the last of the fabric covered models; real stable.

It was so cold the morning we went out that the pilot couldn't get the dipstick out of the engine to check the oil level. We had to put a propane heater under it to thin the oil a bit. Finally we managed to get airborne, and after some navigational difficulties located the property in question.

When we looked down you could see snowmobile tracks leaving the house, going into a bush area, circling and coming back. It was obvious to us that this was his lab or a stash, one of the two. We had been given, for our unique investigation, one of the first Polaroid cameras to be used on the police force, an SX70. If you remember them, when you took the picture it was automatically ejected out the bottom of the camera. The plan was this. The pilot would come in low over a ridge, tilt the plane to my side and slow down. I was to kick the door open and take the pictures.

We flew over a ridge and the pilot slowed the plane. He banked the damn thing so far I thought for sure I was going to fall out into this guy's drug lab and be lost forever. I overcame the panic and stuck the camera out the door. As we passed over the yard I began shooting and I fired off an entire roll of eight shots in quick succession. I pulled the camera back inside with a grin and looked - no pictures! I glanced back behind the plane and there was a confetti-like stream of photographs fluttering gently down right into his yard. Brilliant plan!

***

The call came in on the 9-1-1 line from a lady who was hysterical. Someone was trying to break into her house. We were dispatched and raced to the address - adrenalin flooding our bodies. I loved the catch and I could feel one in my bones tonight. While we were enroute, dispatch kept the woman on the line and relayed to us that she believed the culprit to have entered the basement by now. It's not often you actually catch a bad guy inside a house, and I wasn't letting this one get away from me.

We leapt from the car outside the house and raced to the front door.

The woman, still hysterical, flung the door open and screamed, "He's downstairs, he's downstairs!"

My partner and I sprinted down the steps and exploded into the laundry room. By now we could hear the culprit thumping and thrashing around, and we readied ourselves for either a fight or a foot chase. We quickly searched the room and came up empty-handed, but we could still hear the thumping and scraping. I looked out the basement window and could see a shape near the glass.

"There he is!" I shouted and ran for the stairs.

In a flash I was in the back yard, flashlight in hand, preparing myself for the confrontation. I shone the light on the window area and my heart stopped. There was a skunk ...with it's head caught in a plastic Halloween pumpkin, trying desperately to free itself. I wasn't about to even try arresting it. I hate it when that happens.

***

One night I was working Check Stop on a major route. A car came upon the police vehicles and, as happens in some cases, decided to try and flee. I chased him for a short time and managed to get him stopped. My partner and I placed him under arrest and put him into the back seat of the police van without handcuffing him. This guy was determined he was not going to give us a breath sample. The van is set up in such a way that there is a post behind and between the front seats which contains a locked shotgun and a fire extinguisher. As we returned to the flashing lights of the Check Stop, the guy grabbed the fire extinguisher, stuck the tube in his mouth and pulled the trigger.

Words can't explain the snow storm that took place inside the van. I thought we were in one of those glass ball ornaments with the Christmas scene and the falling snow. There was white powder everywhere. It was over the seats, the dash, the bad guy, us, the windows. I couldn't even see out the windshield to drive so I had to stop. We baled out and took the guy with us. There we stood amid a fog of powder blowing from the vehicle with an arrest who looked like a racoon. Who says Check Stop is boring?

***

Some guys just have days when they never should have gotten out of bed. We got a call one evening to a strange accident involving a motor vehicle at a service station. When we got there we saw a guy sitting between the gas pumps with his head in his hands. He did not look happy. There was a slight skiff of fresh snow, and we could see tire tracks going in great circles all over the lot. We thought we had better listen to his story.

He told us he owned the service station and was leaving to go home when he realized he was out of windshield washer fluid. He pulled up at the pumps and popped the hood, leaving the car running while he went to get a bottle of fluid. When he walked away, the car jumped into gear and, with the choke still on, took off like a shot across the parking lot. The guy tried to climb back in, but the car started to do donuts so he couldn't get near it. It bounced off the front of his garage, breaking out the window and door, then careened into the gas pumps causing major damage. Next it fled across the lot and struck a customer's car that was waiting for a minor tune-up. It then knocked the legs out from under his propane storage tank which fell onto his car, crushing it, and finally bringing the carnage to a halt.

We wrote up the accident and did our best to console the poor fellow. We actually had him feeling a little better when we were done and he was beginning to see the funny side of it all. He got out of the police van and started to walk away. My partner was outside when the guy turned to him.

"By the way," he asked. "You didn't happen to see my glasses anywhere did you?"

I dropped the van into gear and pulled forward.

My partner stooped over and said, "Yes, they're right he ..."

There was a terrible crushing and popping sound of breaking glass followed by a deep moan as the rear wheels of the van flattened his glasses and spewed the shattered remains across the slippery lot.

"Oh well," he said, "Just one of those goddamn days I guess..."

***

When I was in training at the Academy, arrangements were made for the K-9 unit to come and give a talk, along with a practical demonstration of the abilities of the police dogs. The animal presented was a "bomb dog" which, they told us, was used for sniffing out bombs at airports and other buildings.

The handler gave his talk and then it was time for the demonstration. We were all eager to see this wonderful dog perform and were rather excited about the whole idea.

The K-9 guy had a piece of some type of explosive which he had hidden between two stacked chairs at the back of the classroom earlier. He brought the dog into the room and tried to make it sit beside him. The dog went nuts and was really hyper because he wasn't used to so many people in the room.

The handler said, "The dog isn't used to having all these people around, so we'll just let him go sniff all of you first."

He took the dog off the leash and it ran around, licking everybody and getting petted, and just having a wonderful time. He finally called it back and took hold of the collar. With great confidence he gave the command for the dog to search out the bomb and turned him loose. The dog made a little circle in front of the handler, came back, and squatted between the guy's feet where he promptly crapped the biggest pile I have ever seen. In our class book we named him "Aak Aak, The Exploding Bomb Dog!"

***

When we have a person in the back seat of a police car for any reason, part of our job is to gather information.

I had a guy in the car one night and asked him, "Are you working right now?"

"No," he said with some irritation in his voice, "I'm in the back of your lousy police car ...."

***

We found a drunk one night who had walked into a window at a fast food place. The window wasn't broken, he was just standing there with his face against the glass, sleeping. We roused him up and decided to drive him home. My partner was trying to be polite and public-minded so he struck up a conversation with the guy.

"Well," he asked. "How was your night anyway?"

The guy looked at him with that silly grin drunks have and said, "She was u-u-ugly. Why the hell do you think I'm this pissed!"

***

I don't particularly care for snakes, but if I have to deal with them I will. A call was dispatched to us one evening stating a snake was loose in the halls of an apartment building in our area. We responded, and upon arriving at the scene, conducted a floor-by-floor search for what we figured was somebody's pet garter snake. We got to the fourth floor and the elevator door opened quietly. We stepped off and rounded the corner. I was ahead of my partner and we had gone about half way down the hall, when out of the stair well came a twelve foot Boa Constrictor - straight at us.

As one man we turned. It was a fight to see who was going to get into the elevator first. The door finally opened and we both fought our way in as the snake homed in on us. With hearts pounding we pushed the button for the main floor and bolted into the lobby. When we were able to catch our breath we called for animal control to come and give us a hand.

About ten minutes later the officer showed up and got out of the truck with a little stick and loop about eighteen inches long.

I looked at him and said, "You're going to need something bigger than that!"

He turned to me and said, "Listen son, I was doing this when you were still in diapers. I know what I need to do my job. Now show me where this little fella is."

We all got back into the elevator, and up we went to the fourth floor. The door opened and the animal control officer stepped into the hall. We stayed behind and shut the door as quickly as we could. Moments later we heard a frantic pounding on the elevator door and the officer screaming

"Open the door! Open the door!"

"How do I know you're not the snake?" I yelled.

"Fuck off and open the Goddamn door!"

CHAPTER SIX

Hi, Joan here again. I have worked with police officers for most of my career. Over that time I have come to realize that they never tire of practical jokes or seizing an opportunity for a little fun.

One day a constable was walking past the CPIC area and noticed a pair of lacy ladies panties lying on the floor. Not missing a beat he scooped them up with his pen and dangled them over the counter.

"Someone missing something?" he asked with a wry smile.

We all looked and laughed, squirming a little in our seats to make sure we still had everything on that we started the day with. Yup, I was still intact, no problems here, thank God. One of the ladies laughed out loud and said, "I'll bet it was a hooker or someone who was busted last night."

With that, the constable dropped them with finality into the waste basket and left. A little later the same young lady went to thccounter to assist an officer with a warrant, and just as she was turning around she glanced at the panties in the waste basket.

"Oh, my God!" she said, reaching in and plucking them from amid the crumpled papers. She quickly rolled them into a ball and stuffed them into her jeans pocket.

"What's wrong?" I asked.

"These are mine. I washed my jeans last night and they must have got stuck in the leg or something."

"That's okay," I said, "we won't tell anyone." I had my fingers crossed when I made that promise.

The CPIC staff are very conscientious and a great group to work with. We all agree that if it wasn't for a sense of humour our days would be longer and our shifts a lot duller. Days can be bad or days can be good. In some cases though you may have a few warning signs that your day is going to be not so good. Here are a few for you to consider:

"You wake up face-down in the police bar parking lot."

"You arrive at the police station and there is a 60 Minutes film crew waiting for you."

"You want to put on the clothes you wore home from the party last night - but there aren't any."

"Your twin brother forgets your birthday."

"You walk into the locker room and the inspector is waiting for you with your transfer papers."

"The bird singing outside your window is a buzzard."

"Your blind date turned out to be your ex-wife."

"Your shift colleagues have a birthday cake for you, and the fire department is standing by while they light the candles."

I always manage to glean a few of the more important ideas from the officers who come to the CPIC counter. Here are a few gems of wisdom they have left me with over the years:

"If the sergeant's plan was stupid but it worked, it wasn't stupid."

"The house you are ignoring at a major incident is probably the house where the bad guy really is."

"Pepper spray works on cops too and regardless of the wind direction will always blow back into your face."

"A successful conclusion to a major incident is just the place where the sergeant ran out of ideas."

Just before we get on with the real stories here I would like to offer a "tongue-in-cheek" view of the chain of command:

The Deputy Chief:	Leaps not-so-tall buildings with a single bound; is as fast as a speeding bullet; slows down locomotives with bare hands; occasionally talks to God.
The Superintendent:	Leaps small buildings with a single bound; is slower than a speeding bullet; has on occasion slowed down a small truck; seldom talks to God.
The Inspector:	Jumped over a small house once; is not allowed to play with guns; slows down standard-sized automobiles with bare hands; God, on occasion, talks to him.
The Sergeant:	Jumps over one-storey houses in two bounds; slow at reaching for dinner checks; stopped a VW once; God speaks to him if there is no-one else around.
The Street Cop:	Lifts tall buildings with one hand and walks under them; grabs speeding bullets and eats

	them; stops locomotives with a wave of the hand; considered by some to be God.
The Rookie:	Jumps into the air and slams into walls at lower than window level; gets the safety off the shotgun in six deft tries; not allowed to play alone on the streets; God just shakes his head.

Okay, enough shots already! Let's get on with more of the really good stuff.

***

I had to pee one night so bad I thought I was going to explode. We were at a house where the people didn't really like the police, so I wasn't going to ask them to use their bathroom. The call took an hour and I was in agony by the time we left. My partner headed the car for our district office and I crossed my legs. God I was in bad shape. We were almost there when a house alarm came in and there was no other car to attend. The dispatcher assigned it to us and we had to go. I knew I was going to explode.

The house we arrived at was one of those big shacks in the better part of town. The residents were away and the keyholder let us in to search the premises. The alarm system was one that was connected to a monitoring station as well as having a horn on scene. My partner went to the basement while I went upstairs. I cleared the rooms one by one, and as I reached the end of the hall I saw the bathroom. My bladder refused to retain its contents any longer. I slipped quietly into the room and closed the door. I undid my fly and was letting forth a tremendous stream when the alarm went off again. The horn was in the bathroom right behind me.

Well, there was piss from ceiling to floor. I sprayed up the shower curtains, across the sink, over the floor tiles, and onto the door as I spun around to see what the hell was going on. When I regained my composure I realized I had pissed all over myself. My uniform was soaked. I cleaned the mess and went back downstairs to where my partner was waiting.

"Take me home!" I said.

"Why?" he asked.

"Never mind, just take me home!"

As it turned out another emergency call came in and we had to attend. By the time we finished I smelled like a urinal in a cheap hotel.

***

We had a hard working staff sergeant in Drugs who liked to come on busts with the guys to keep informed. He was a pretty big guy and was always right up at the front lines when the action started. We had to take down an apartment one night and the staff came with us, eager for action. There was a long hall which came to a "T" and our suspect's door was right at the "T", facing us.

The staff decided he was going to take down the door and show his men how it was supposed to be done. He tore off down the hall on a dead run - like a football linebacker -with his shoulder down and forward. He hit the door hard, expecting it to shatter at the lock. It was unlatched and it exploded open with a reverberating "Twwwaaannngggg!!!!" The staff flew into the apartment at warp speed and tripped on a scatter rug. He did a complete somersault and vaulted unceremoniously into the living room where he landed heavily on his back under the coffee table. He really winded himself in the process! As we arrived at the door, his hand, holding his badge, slithered up from under the table.

"C-c-city Police," he said, trying to catch his breath, "you're all ... under ... arrest."

The pot heads were all staring at the disembodied hand and badge, their eyes trying to focus.

"Far out," one of them said. "This is heavy man, like where's the rest of him, this must be good shit man."

***

A long time ago policemen weren't very well paid and quite a few of us had second jobs. We weren't supposed to be moonlighting but, to make a few extra bucks and stay in shape, we used to unload boxcars. We'd get about ten guys and make a chain gang to unload cases of Campbell's soup or hundred-pound bags of flour or whatever they had for us. We would work night shift, then go to work on the moonlighting job all day and then work

**"WADDYA MEAN YOU'VE LOST
YOUR SENSE OF PURPOSE?"**

the night shift again.

We had done this for a few days in a row and were getting pretty ragged. We showed up for night shift and had a quiet watch. The Albertan truck delivered the morning paper about five-thirty, so we pulled up to the bus stop and my partner got a paper. He took the sports section, gave me the rest, and we sat there at the bus stop in the police car reading the paper. It was abou quarter to six in the morning when I looked over at him. He was starting to doze off and in no time at all his head was buried in the paper. Seconds later he was sound asleep.

I kept on reading and sure enough my eyelids got a little heavy. I blinked and I woke up about half an hour later. I shook my head and looked around to see six people standing at the bus stop. My partner still had his face planted in the sports page and I was peeking out from under the comics. Pretending nothing was abnormal, I threw my paper over my partner's head, dropped the car into gear and drove away. Thank God we didn't have numbers on the side of the cars in those days.

There was a time when we were supposed to eat our lunch at Haddon Hall. We'd go in around three or three-thirty in the morning and brown bag it. While we were having lunch, a car crew, somehow, came across a big Rhode Island Red chicken. They snuck it into the back seat of our patrol car.

We finished our break and drove away to check some industrial properties. The chicken was asleep in the back seat and we never noticed it. We drove through the industrial area and didn't see so much as a mouse moving. We decided to get a paper and read through it. We got the morning Albertan and found a quiet alley where we parked to peruse the headlines. After we finished we decided to grab about twenty minutes shut-eye before we booked off for the nightI tossed the paper into the back seat and we nestled down for a snooze. I had just closed my eyes when I heard a rustling on the paper.

"Settle down," I said to my partner. "You're keeping me awake."

"It's not me," he said.

We turned simultaneously to see what the hell the noise was. As we leaned over the seat the chicken came fully awake and flew into our faces like a shot from a cannon. There were screams and flailing arms and shouts and feathers all over the damned place. The chicken landed on the dash and then careened back at me. It bounced off my face and jumped onto my partner's shoulder. He hit the thing with a back-hander and finally knocked it into the rear seat where we were able to grab it. Our hearts were going a hundred miles an hour and our suits were covered in chicken shit. We looked like something from a Ma and Pa Kettle movie.

This was too good to let slide. Now we had this chicken and we were determined to get someone else. We drove to headquarters where a young lady by the name of Rosie worked in the Warrants Section. Rosie had a routine every morning. She would come in, hang up her hat and coat on the rack, go to her desk, open the top drawer and put her purse inside. So we put the chicken into the drawer of her desk, tucked it down carefully, and closed the drawer tight. Then we hid around the corner.

Sure enough, Rosie came in and followed her routine. She hung up her hat and coat, went to her desk, and reached for the drawer. When she opened it, the chicken came out screeching and flapping like a banshee, glanced off her forehead and shot eight feet into the air. Rosie screamed and ran out of the office, flailing her arms just like the chicken. In a few minutes she came back, picked up her hat, coat and purse, and took the rest of the day off.

***

I used to be dispatcher back in the old days when one guy would look after the entire city for a shift. I was the only one on the board and when it got busy you didn't have time for anything. I got a call one night from a guy who had found a snake in his apartment. I sent a car crew over to collect the thing and dispose of it at the zoo or whatever. When they got there they found a very large Boa Constrictor which had got loose in one apartment and gone through the vents into another. It was sleeping on the guy's bed. The constables grabbed a large laundery bag and stuffed the snake inside.

In those days when you made an arrest, you would stop by my dispatch office and tell me you had an arrest and would be off the air for awhile. So it was no big deal when these two constables came into the office. They told me they had an arrest and asked me if I would mind keeping an eye on this bag for them.

I was really busy on the dispatch terminal but said, "Sure, just toss it on the desk there."

They did and left. While I was giving out calls to the car crews, out of the corner of my eye I thought I saw the bag move. I kept answering calls and dispatching in a flurry of activity until I saw the bag move again. Now

I had to see what was in it. I wheeled my chair over to the desk and ripped open the top of the bag. The snake lunged out of the bag and we were eyeball to eyeball. I pushed my chair back so fast it fell over, and I rolled in a complete somersault. I landed on my feet, already running, and made it to the office door in a single leap where I was met by the entire night shift crew.

***

Dispatching used to be a plum job. We had only four 9-1-1 lines and about eight lines for the general calls which were manned by four constables. They would take the information, write it down, and pass it on to the dispatcher. I was asked to come in and help out on the phones one night, so I did and in no time I was onto the system. It got really busy, and I was wrapped up in what I was doing. The emergency light came on at the 9-1-1 line so I grabbed it.

"City Police Emergency, can I help you?"

A voice said, "Get here fast, they're stuffing bodies right into the furnace!"

"Sir, sir, give me your name and address."

It's the white house - on the corner."

"That won't do sir, what is your address?"

He hollered into the phone, "It's right

across ... Oh! There goes another body into the furnace. This is terrible! Send help please!!!"

By now I was panicking and looking around the control room for some help. It was then I noticed that I was the only one there. I looked over to the small outer office and there was my shift supervisor on the outside line talking to me. The entire communications crew was crouched down behind his desk laughing. I've never answered a 9-1-1 call since then without thinking about that.

***

I was teaching P.T. down in the police gym. I took a lot of pride at staying in good shape, and I used to take the class of about fifty guys out for a morning run. Before we went we did stretching and warm-ups in the gym. This particular morning we were doing jumping jacks where you clap above your head and then land on your feet.

I hollered, "C'mon you guys! You're like a bunch of old farts, let's go - one, two, one, two, one two," at a real good pace.

I guess I got a little over-enthused, and on "two" my upper denture came flying out of my mouth. It sailed about ten feet in the air and straight into the middle of the group. The class immediately went into hysterics and fell to the floor. I managed to retrieve my teeth, but I think I lost control of the class for the day.

***

I used to have one of those partners who was a self-professed expert on everything possible. There was nothing he didn't know about anything, and he had done it first or better than anyone else. I was new on the job so I took this guy at his word. As a matter of fact, I looked up to his knowledge.

I figured, "Now here's a guy I can learn from!"

As it turned out he didn't know shit from chewing tobacco.

One day we were asked to check out a report of a bomb at a phone booth. Of course, my partner was also the resident expert on bombs. We arrived at the phone booth and took a look inside. There sat a white, World War II shell about three feet high and six inches across.

My partner, the expert, said, "We don't have to worry because white is used to denote a dummy shell. There is no danger whatsoever."

What he neglected was the fact that there

"NOW CUT THE RED WIRE.. NO, HANG ON, THE WHITE WIRE,
... NOT THE RED WIRE, CUT THE WHITE WIRE... HELLO... HELLO!..."

BOMB DISPOSAL OFFICER

was a bunch of wires running all over this thing with holes drilled in it and things taped to it and gadgets on it. In addition, the origi nal shell was still sticking out of the top of the casing.

However, he reassured me that there was absolutely no danger.

He said, "Pick it up and put it into the car."

Being very young and very green, I accepted his supposed expertise and picked the damned thing up. I walked over to the car and got in, placing the shell on the front seat between my legs.

We drove to Sarcee Military Barracks to meet with the M.P.'s. They took us to the bomb range where they said they would wire it up and blow it for us. By now I had the utmost confidence in my senior partner, and was flipping the shell around like it was only a piece of wood or something. I wasn't the least bit worried.

We put it into a sand pit that was barricaded with logs and rocks, and we watched as the demolition expert from the army put a little plastic explosive on the outside of the shell. He ran two wires and we stood back about fifty yards inside a bunker.

He said, "Now when I hook this thing up, there will be a little pop, just enough to ensure us that there's no danger. There's nothing to worry about." (Another expert!)

We squatted down and the guy made the connection on his battery. What followed was the most gawdawful explosion one man ever told another about. It sent sand bags, logs and rocks flying all over hell's half acre. There was smoke and stones and wood chips falling from two hundred feet in the air. If that thing had gone off in the car parts of my anatomy would have landed in Lethbridge. I never believed another word that asshole told me.

***

It was hot! I mean it was really hot, and I was driving along thinking about a beer at the end of my shift. I looked up the road and saw a car off to the side with the hood up. About a block away the driver was walking with a gas can in his hand. I decided it was time to show the citizens that this was the Calgary Police "SERVICE". I was going to give this guy a lift to the gas station and help him get his car going again.

I pulled the police car alongside the fellow and said, "Hop in, I'll give you a ride to the gas station."

He said, "No thanks," and kept on walking.

Like I said, it was really hot and the

guy was a little older. I was worried about him maybe taking a heat stroke or something, so I insisted.

"Come on, get in and I'll give you a lift."

"No!" he replied with fervour and kept on walking.

I pulled the car beside him again and flung the passenger door open. As I did, he leaned over to say something, and I struck him on the top of the head with the edge of the door. It opened a gash about three inches long on his scalp and he started to bleed profusely. I jumped out of the car and helped him into the front seat. We rushed to the hospital. After I took him inside with his gas can, I decided I should go back and help with his car. By the time I returned to the scene it had been towed by someone else. So much for the police "SERVICE " aspect.

***

We don't often get calls of prowlers on the roofs of apartment buildings, but this one came in and we decided to take a look at it. We arrived at the building and went to the apartment on the top floor from which the complaint had originated.

I rang the bell and a woman in slacks and a heavy knit sweater answered the door.

She had an absolutely huge pair of breasts, and from the way they moved around she wasn't wearing a bra. Keeping a proper professional attitude we listened as she told us the problem, and then took us to the little room that allowed access to the roof. We all went inside and closed the door. In the centre of the room was a metal ladder that went up to the roof hatch. The room itself was no more than four feet by four feet and we were all crammed inside.

The ladder was between my partner and me and the lady was standing behind me with her back pressed against the wall. I decided I would climb the ladder and take a look. I got up about four steps when the lady reached out and grabbed my ass. I brushed her hand away and tried to keep going. She grabbed my ass again and tried to pull me down. I thought, "What the hell is going on, and my partner is doing nothing?"

I looked down and he was standing there with his mouth open and eyes wide. When I started up the ladder my gun handle caught in her knit sweater and it was up around her neck. My partner thanked me for months.

***

About twelve of us went to a poolparty at a friend's apartment one night after shift.

We proceeded to drink and enjoy ourselves and ss luck would have it, we all ended up in the pool. When we got out we went down to the laundry room to put our clothes in the dryer and have a few more beers. We peeled our clothes off and tossed them into the machine. One of the guys found some dresses, an apron, and some ladies underwear. We decided that rather than be naked we would don these articles, but we would turn the lights off in case someone wandered by. Things were fine for a bit, and then suddenly a woman came around the corner and flipped the lights on. Here were these half-naked men, twelve of us, some in women's clothing, sitting all over the room.

The first thing that came out of my mouth was, "It's okay lady, we're all policemen".

I don't know if she's ever trusted a cop since.

***

For the most part, policemen are just regular guys. The only problem with them is that they tend to trust their cohorts a little too much at times. Quite a while ago a princess from India was visiting Calgary, and while she was here, someone had the gall to steal her fur coat. Some time later I was searching a house belonging to a bunch of druggies, and my partner came out of the bedroom with the fur coat belonging to the princess. He thought nothing of it and saw that it was returned to the owner in due course.

Weeks later an envoy arrived at the office with a package for my partner. When he opened it he found a beautiful statue that was a family heirloom belonging to the princess. He was instructed by the envoy that it was his reward for having recovered the princess' coat. He tried to refuse, but was told it would be an insult to do so. You have never seen anybody so proud of something in your life. He took it around, showed it off to everybody, and was as happy as could be.

That night I went back to the office and got into his locker with a spare key. I had pulled a sticker off one of my kids toys that was made in Taiwan, and I stuck it on the bottom of the statue.

Next day I came to work and met my partner. I told him I wanted to see the statue again and he went to get it. The whole office gathered round as he came back and stood in front of me grinning from ear to ear.

"That's very nice," I said, taking the statue and turning it over. "But what's this? Made in Taiwan?"

He grabbed the statue from me with fire in his eyes and turned it upside down.

"What the hell?" he yelled and tossed it

into the garbage can.

He was pissed off at me for weeks before he could see the funny side of it.

***

I was in Traffic Enforcement and loved to ride the Harleys. We were the stars of the Stampede Parade every year, and it took us an entire shift to get ready. We spent half a shift polishing leather and helmets, and the other half hand-waxing our motorcycles. Talk about spit and polish - we were it!

The morning of the parade we were getting ready to do our thing. I had my bike out and did the final dusting and checking for fingerprints. It was without blemish and I was gloating. We had an hour before the parade so a few of us decided to go for a short ride to loosen up a bit. We rode into the morning sun like knights in armour, all clean and glistening. What a sight we were!

We hadn't gone ten blocks when a call came in that one of the Stampede Parade horses had gotten loose and was in traffic on a major road. We all decided to head over there and see if we could corral it with our bikes.

The horse was in traffic all right and had it snarled pretty good. We worked our way towards the frightened animal, and I guess the sound of the bikes spooked it because he took off like a flash. Three of us gave chase as the horse ran up over an embankment. I followed on my bike, accelerating gracefully as I reached the crest of the hill. As I got to the top my bike found traction on the slippery grass and it launched over the crest of the hill. The horse stopped and I shot right past it ... into the biggest, deepest, muddiest quagmire you ever saw.

I was right in the middle when the damned thing stalled. I had no choice. Down went my polished motorcycle boots right up over my ankles into the soupy mud. The bike kicked in again and I had the throttle wide open. The rear wheel threw mud twenty feet in the air and I was instantly covered from head to foot. Then the damned thing coughed its last and quit.

I pushed the bike out and got it started. Just as I was about to head back to the garage to wash up our Sergeant called us to meet him at the Parade Route.

I was the star attraction as we rode. Mr. Mud!!!!!

CHAPTER SEVEN

I'll bet by now you're all feeling really safe out there. What with policemen falling off their motorcycles, getting locked in their own cars, diving into swimming pools, and shooting mannequins; I'm sure you will all sleep better at night.

It's not just the street constables who get themselves into hilarious situations. Our TAPS (Telephone Answering Personnel) do just as well. These are the real front-line people who work in the Communications Centre. They take the calls from the public and pass them on to the dispatchers for assignment to car crews ... if the call gets that far!

To explain what I mean, let's listen in on a few 9-1-1 calls:

"City Police Emergency."

"Hullo ... need to make complaint please."

"What is the complaint, sir?"

"Am receiving phone call from person asking about our bomb. Is saying scary things."

"What did the caller say about the bomb, sir?"

The TAPS was already sending the preliminary bomb threat information to the dispatcher.

"He say he watch my wife and she has a nice bomb! I want to complain."

***

"City Police Emergency."

"Hi. I paid a hooker fifty dollars for a blow job but she didn't do it. She jumped into a car and drove away. What can I do about it?"

"This really isn't a police matter, sir. It's something you'll have to work out with the young lady if you ever see her again."

"Okay, but that's not all."

"Yes, sir. What else happened?"

"I had to pee so I stopped into this gay bar just to use the washroom ..."

"Yes, sir."

"Well, while I was there I noticed that they were serving drinks in those glass mason jars. So I went to the bouncer and asked him why they served their liquor in old fruit jars. How badly do you have to be beaten up to press assault charges?"

***

"Dispatch to 1153."

"Go ahead."

"Can you begin making your way to the Keen Hotel? We have a guy on the E-line who claims there are three dead bodies on the ninth floor. He isn't sure which room."

"10-4, we're on the way."

"1101," she called the district sergeant.

"Go ahead," he responded.

"Did you copy we have a possible homicide at the Keen Hotel? 1153 is enroute."

"10-4, I'll start that way too."

"10-4. Do I have a unit to back up 1153 at a possible homicide?"

"1111, send it to us, we'll go."

"10-4, ... all units on the possible homicide stand-by for an update ... 1101, 1153 and 1111, you can stand down. The caller just stated he was watching this with his friend who is invisible!"

***

"City Police, how can I help you?"

"Hi, I want to complain about a terribly loud stereo coming from the house behind me."

"Yes ma'am. What's the address?"

"I'm not sure, but it's easy to find."

"Why's that, ma'am?"

"Because it has a big sign that says Half-Way House for the Deaf!"

***

"City Police Emergency."

"I'm leaving my apartment now!"

"I'm sorry, but I don't know what you're talking about."

"Could I speak to someone who would know then?"

"Try explaining it a little better to me."

"Can I talk to someone who knows? If you don't know what's the point in talking to you?"

"I don't have a clue what you're talking about!"

"I don't want you to have a clue. I wish to speak to another policeman who might have a clue."

"What is your problem?"

"It's none of your business!"

"Listen, you called me - now what is your problem???"

"That's right! I am a citizen!! I'm trying to tell you that if you don't listen then what's the point?"

Bang!!! The caller hung up.

***

"City Police Emergency."

"My sister and I are home alone and there is a guy on the ladder trying to get in our front window. Send somebody please!!!"

"Okay, a car is on the way. Just stay on the line with me and try to stay calm."

"Hurry, he's on the ladder at the front door now. I think he's trying to pick the lock. I'm really scared!!"

"I know, I know. The police will be there in a minute or so. Don't hang up."

"He's been trying to get in for about an hour. He's banging on the door! Now he's trying to saw the door handle off ... please hurry!!!"

"It won't be long now, just stay with me."

"Now he has a bar or something! He's going up on the roof ... now he's drilling the roof!!! Oh good, the police car is here now."

"1223 to dispatch."

"Go ahead, 1223."

"Tell the kids it's only their dad putting up the Christmas lights."

***

"City Police, can I help you?"

"Hello, I'm from out of town and I just had an accident."

"Yes, sir."

"I was driving eastbound in second gear and went through the intersection on a red light. I was just following the rest of the traffic and believed I was driving in the normal Calgarian fashion."

***

Non-emergency calls at the Comm. Centre deserve some attention as well:

"City Police, how can I help you?"

"My neighbour's dog barked all last night, woof, woof, woof, woof, woof."

"Uh-huh."

"And it's still barking this morning, woof, woof, woof, woof, woof."

"Mm-hmm."

"And it won't stop, woof, woof, woof, woof, woof."

"This is a German Shepherd, right?"

"Right, how did you know that? Has someone else complained?"

"No, sir, it was just something in your voice."

***

"1142."

"Go ahead."

"We have a complaint of a man who has been sitting on the front steps of Sam's Bingo Hall for about three hours. Can you slide around there and check him out, please?"

"10-4."

(A few minutes later.)

"1142 is out. He's still here. I'll let you know."

(Pause.)

"1142 to dispatch."

"Go ahead."

"He was waiting for the bingo hall to open. We pointed out to him that it was June and there was a big sign on the door saying - closed for renovations until July 30. He's gone home now."

Okay, back to the street!

***

I stole my staff sergeant's lunch and put three rubber play worms in his sandwich. I knew when he was taking his lunch break and a bunch of us went to the cafeteria to watch the fun. Sure enough the staff came in right on time, followed by his superintendent. They sat down near us, and from their voices we could tell they were discussing something very serious. The superintendent was just making what appeared to be an extremely

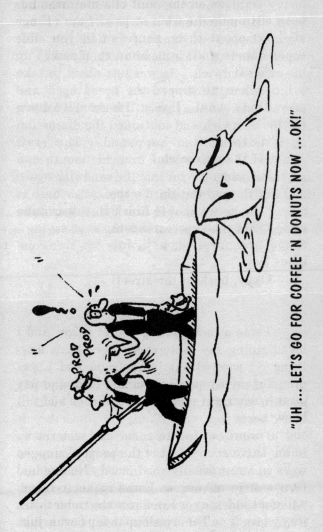

"UH ... LET'S GO FOR COFFEE 'N DONUTS NOW ...OK!"

heavy point when the staff bit into his sandwich. He pulled back and two of the rubber worms flopped out, dangling from his lips. The superintendent sat a moment, then picked up his own sandwich. He was just about to take a bite when he flipped the bread open and peered between the layers. He chomped down on the sandwich and continued the discussion as if nothing had happened. The staff removed the two worms from his mouth and set them aside. He bit into the sandwich again and out flopped the third worm.

"Maybe we should finish this discussion later," said the superintendent.

***

I was a cocky young traffic officer and I loved riding my motorcycle more than anything. I worked out in the gym and I was proud of my shape. I thought I looked pretty good in my tight motorcycle breeches and tall black boots.

I went out to run radar and was set up in an active spot. Most of the people I stopped were in an unusually good mood. No one had torn a strip off me, so I was rather relaxed. All of a sudden a car came into the radar beam flying low. I pulled myself up to my best height and stepped onto the roadway. In a moment I had the vehicle stopped and noticed a very pretty girl was driving.

Deciding to try a somewhat different and cool approach, I strode to the car and hooked my thumbs into the belt of my uniform.

Looking out from under the brim of my gleaming helmet I said, "Well, sweetheart, where's the fire?"

She looked up at me without batting an eye and said, "Under my ass big boy. Have you got a hose long enough to put it out?"

***

Statements come from all types of witnesses, and under stressful conditions they may be somewhat disjointed. Here is one from a bank robbery that kind of says it all.

"Heard the shot ... hit the floor ... saw no more!"

***

I was working at the front counter of police headquarters when a guy came in looking very lost.

I stood and asked him, "Can I help you sir?"

"I think so," he said, looking over his shoulder like he was expecting someone to jump him from behind.

"What seems to be the problem?"

"Well, uh, I parked my car this morning and now I can't seem to find it," he said.

"That's not a problem sir," I said. "It may have been towed for parking or such. I'll call the impound lot and check for you."

"Uh, there's more," he continued. "You see, the building ... the one I parked my car beside ... well ... it's ... gone too."

I was about to call for the guys in the white coats when two officers walked into the lobby.

"Wow," one said. "You shoulda seen that old hotel fall. It went down like a deck of cards. Those demolition guys sure know their stuff."

I turned back to the guy without the car and never missed a beat.

"Of course," I said as if I knew all along, "the building was demolished, didn't you know? I'm sure they towed your vehicle for safety."

***

High Court is very serious. They deal with all the heavy cases and no one has much of a sense of humour there. I'm a female officer and was subpoenaed as investigating constable on a fatal accident. The case was very dry. I gave my evidence and was waiting for my partner to be called to the stand.

We had been sitting for about an hour when he turned to me and said, "I have to take a whiz. Would you watch my diagrams for me?"

"Sure," I said with a grin.

He was a traffic reconstructionist and was going to be giving expert evidence regarding crash dynamics, measurements of skid marks, co-efficient of friction, and all that other stuff reconstructionists know about. The judge puts a lot of weight on his evidence.

The diagrams are in a round plastic tube about three feet long and four inches across. There is a cap that screws onto one end to keep the papers inside. I tore off to the ladies room and quickly slipped out of my uniform top. I pulled off my bra and slid it down into the middle of the rolled-up diagrams. I was careful to stick the fastening hooks over the top end of the papers, and then I replaced the screw top. I redressed and quickly returned to the bench outside the court.

I was sitting there innocently when he came back from the washroom. As he arrived the court officer opened the door and called him to the stand. I followed him into the room and took a seat.

The prosecutor asked him some very pointed questions and he gave all the right answers. My partner was very well educated and well-spoken in court. No one had been able to shake him on the stand yet.

"Did you make scale diagrams of the accident scene?" the prosecutor asked.

"Yes, sir I did," he responded proudly.

"Would you please produce them for the court?"

Without a flinch he opened the end of the tube and snapped the papers out with a practiced flick. His jaw dropped to the floor as the bra flew out of the midst of the papers and landed square on the judge's desk in front of him. The judge studied the item for a moment and then pushed it back across the desk with his pencil. My partner grabbed the bra and stuffed it back into the tube.

The judge called a "brief" recess and that finished everyone off. It took nearly a half an hour to get everyone to stop laughing long enough to recall court.

***

As a policewoman I can honestly say that I have never fallen back on my sex in order to accomplish my job ... well, almost never.

I was downtown one day with my partner. We were just leaving headquarters when a desperate call came over the air from a constable who was obviously in a serious fight. We were close and responded quickly. As luck would have it we were the first car out at the scene. We found two of the biggest, strongest policemen we had ever met fighting wildly with two of the biggest, strongest drunks we had ever seen. The officers were slowly losing the battle and needed help badly.

I stepped from the police car and was about to holler "Stop!" when the fighting suddenly came to an end. Both of the large gentlemen dumped the policemen onto the pavement and came to stand in front of me. One of them looked at me a moment and I was sure I was going to die. His head swayed from alcohol but he smiled widely.

"You're beautiful," he said.

By this time the two officers were getting up from the ground and dusting themselves off.

One of the combatants looked at them and asked, "Can she arrest us? If she can we'll go with her."

Taking my cue, I went to the back of the paddy wagon and opened the door. Both of the gentlemen followed quietly and got in of their own accord. As I was closing the rear compartment, one of the guys leaned forward.

"Do you date?" he asked.

I just smiled demurely and closed the door. I decided to follow the wagon to headquarters in case they acted up again. When the officers opened the van doors, one of the arrestees passed me a piece of paper with both of their names on it.

"Thanks," I said, "but I never mix business with pleasure."

***

Dignity towards the dead is never a question, but sometimes it just doesn't happen that way. This was the first time I attended a sudden death on the job. I was working alone so it was up to me to make sure that all the needs of the family were met. I also had to ensure that the body was properly taken care of in a discreet manner.

The deceased lady was elderly and quite heavy. We had some measure of difficulty getting her out of the basement suite. The body removal company had only sent one guy and I was helping him. It was a tough job but we finally managed to bring her up the stairs into the crisp, winter daylight.

The Medical Examiner was with us and she was walking beside me, asking a few final questions as we worked our way towards the black body van at the curb. The sidewalks were covered in a skiff of snow over ice and walking was difficult. As we neared the van, I lost my footing and my leg shot out from under me. I flailed my foot to the side in an attempt to maintain my balance, and in doing so I kicked the Medical Examiner right on that little round bone on the side of her ankle. I guess the pain was excruciating because she dropped her briefcase, grabbed her ankle, and danced across the lawn. She was howling like a banshee, but I was too involved in trying to save my own balance to notice much.

I was doing a soft shoe shuffle on the ice and juggling the stretcher. I was staring into the body remover's face with this ridiculous "help me" look when I finally lost it. Down I went, right on top of the body. The body removal guy set his end of the stretcher down and was trying to maintain his composure as he looked at the two of us.

"Roll off, you fool," he yelled.

I did ... just as the M.E. went bouncing past on one leg. I took her foot out from under her and she fell right on top of me face-to-face.

"Can't you come up with a better line than this for meeting women," she chuckled.

Neither of them have ever asked me to help move a body again.

***

Motorcycle cops are a breed unto themselves. We are the macho men of Traffic. We are the envy of the police force on warm summer days. Ar, ar!

I had the world by the ass and I was cruising. The sun was on my face, the wind in my ears, and a car on my right. The sun and wind remained constant, but the car made an abrupt turn across the lane in front of me. In a flash I was down, sliding along the street with the greatest show of sparks you've ever seen. Hell, I was even having an accident in style.

I wasn't hurt even though I wore a hole right through my new motorcycle pants. People came from all over to see if I was okay, but I maintained my macho image and refused their assistance.

"I'm not injured," I said. "I'm a trained rider."

The accident was investigated and the driver charged. She plead not guilty and I was subpoenaed to court. When I arrived I strutted to the stand, motorcycle helmet clutched just so under my arm. I was tall and just aloof enough to set myself apart from the other officers in the court. Not enough to be ignorant, you had to know how to balance yourself with others. I gave the evidence with my best court voice and stepped from the witness box with just the right air of self-confidence and cock-sureness.

Now it was the lady's turn to give evidence. She approached the stand very nervously. She told her side and was being cross-examined by the Crown Prosecutor when there developed some question as to whether or not the headlight of the motorcycle was off or on.

The Crown asked her, "Well then, what was the first thing you said when you realized you had had an accident?"

She thought for a brief moment and then said in a loud voice, "Oh my God, I just hit a little boy on a scooter!!!"

In one sentence she had managed to knock every peg out from under me that I had worked so hard to put there. Oh well ... pride cometh!

***

Part of the service offered to the public is the assistance of police at large funerals in order to keep the procession together. We are to be on our best behaviour and to show the utmost respect at all times. I was on such a detail one day and my partner pulled the police car into an intersection to stop traffic. I jumped out and was about to start directing vehicles when my partner drove the car onto my foot.

Just then the funeral procession arrived. I was in great pain and was waving frantically with both arms at my partner. I yelled at him right when the family car passed and

Tales from the Police Locker room Vol. 1

182

was still waving like a circus chimpanzee. They waved back politely and smiled, you know that 'polite' smile that silently says, "I have no idea what you are doing or why you are doing it and I don't want to know!"

***

It was a few years - no, a lot of years ago when I was a rookie. I had a good partner who was a little older than myself. He always teased me about my fishing, and told me if I paid as much attention to women as I paid to fishing, I'd make some woman very happy. In those days we wore long tunics as winter dress and there were military style buttons on the sleeves.

He and I were in the cafeteria when a new CPIC woman came in to have lunch. I made a comment to my partner, which was the wrong thing to do. I was very shy. My partner never missed a beat. He stood, walked over to her, leaned down, said something, and left.

I crumpled up my lunch bag and went to the garbage can. Just as I was stuffing the bag into the old-style swing-lid on the trash can, the woman spoke to me. I was flabbergasted and drove my arm deep into the garbage can. I was trying to be cool and make a decent exit when I turned to walk away. The lid closed on my arm, caught on the metal sleeve buttons, and I picked up the whole can. There I was, banging and clanging towards the door with the lunchroom garbage can hanging on my arm. I never did find out what she said. I never had the nerve to talk to her again.

***

At times in our duties we find it necessary to attend the morgue for one reason or another. We had to go there to follow up on a case, and when we arrived we were told that a recruit class was coming through for their orientation. The staff was busy and asked if I would mind showing the rookies around. No problem!

They were all waiting out front in their nicely pressed uniforms, and involved in nervous chatter as I went out to greet them.

I took the class in, keeping my voice very low and quiet. I was giving them all kinds of creepy details about bodies and the morgue itself. They were intrigued and their eyes were like saucers the whole time. I had them right in the palm of my hand.

We finally arrived at the body fridge where we stepped inside. I showed them a corpse or two and had them look closely at the injuries to determine what the cause of death might have been; traffic accident, natural, homicide, all very professional. They hung onto my every word.

I finally got to a slab with a covered corpse on it and slapped the body on the chest. "Well, Bob, how are we today?" I asked.

"Fine!" my partner yelled at the top of his voice and bolted up.

What followed was a mass of twenty recruits trying to get through a single door all at once.

***

I had to deliver a subpoena one day to a guy who lived right next door to a college. It was lunch time and I think every student in the school was outside. I was in the Motorcycle Division at the time and felt the same as most guys do there, macho and cool, especially when people gathered around to admire your bike.

I pulled up in front of the residence and immediately a group gathered around me before I dismounted. They asked me questions about the bike and being on the force. I was enjoying the attention.

After a bit I said, "I have police work to do," and dismounted.

What I had omitted to do was put the kickstand down. As I walked away, the bike fell towards me. Bad enough it fell, but the handlebar caught me in the back of the knee and I went down like a dishrag. I landed on my face right at their feet, my helmet bouncing off the pavement like a dropped nickel. I stood up, dusted myself off, picked up the bike and rode quietly away. So much for macho!

***

I was dispatched to an injury accident which took place on a major thoroughfare. When I arrived I found the scene to be actually on a bridge which had three lanes in each direction. The roadway was divided by cement GM barriers and a swift flowing river passed under the concrete.

The collision was not very serious so I was able to handle the scene by myself. Both parties were taken to hospital, and the paperwork was almost finished. I was sitting in the car putting the final touches on the accident diagram and waiting for the tow trucks to arrive. I had been at the scene for about thirty-five minutes when I spotted a guy running along the side of the road towards my police car. He was soaking wet and covered in mud and seaweed from head to toe.

As he approached my car he started yelling and waving his hands. I rolled down my window and waited.

He ran up to the car and yelled, "I saw the accident, I saw the accident!"

I looked him over carefully and then asked, "You mean this accident?"

"Yes, yes," he yelled. "I'm a witness. I want to give you a statement."

"That's fine, sir, but might I ask ... where have you been, the accident happened over half an hour ago?"

"I was on the other side of the highway," he yelled, waving his arms around and splashing water all over me. "When I saw the accident I stopped and ran over to see if I could help. I jumped over the barriers there in the middle of the road. Do you know there's a big hole in there? I fell thirty-five feet into the damned river. I was swept about two miles downstream and it took me this long to get back. Where do I write my statement?"

Now that's civic duty!!!

***

We were driving down an alley one day when we saw a kid with one of those expensive slingshots. I guess he didn't see us because he loaded up a ball bearing and let it fly at a car window. Boom! There was glass everywhere.

We were on him like dirty shorts and arrested him on the spot. We charged him and seized the slingshot for evidence. We had to take it to the property room to enter as an exhibit, and while we were driving my partner was testing its power.

He pulled it back and forth and said, "These things are damned dangerous! There's a lot of power in this rubber."

He dug into the bag of ball bearings we had also seized and took one out.

"I wonder how far it'll go?" he asked as he loaded the round into the leather on the rubber band.

He leaned back in his seat, pointed the slingshot towards a field, and let fly the steel ball. Boom! There was glass everywhere.

When my heart stopped pounding I turned to him and said, "They go farther if you roll the window down."

CHAPTER EIGHT

April Fools Day! My, what a wonderful day to be at work on the police department. This is a fun day, a time of laughter, frivolity, chagrin, mirth ... making a complete fool of yourself! I have never been a practical joker, but I decided that CPIC needed a little more life, so I would help things out. A woman on our shift was a joker and played many tricks on all of us. I saw the perfect opportunity to get her back ... at least I thought I did. What's the expression? Never scam a scammer!

She was dating a police officer from out of town and made arrangements to meet him in Vernon, British Columbia, on the weekend. I made up a CPIC message and typed it on our special paper stating her guy was cancelling the weekend. I was going to give it to her, let her react, and then we could laugh together.

When she arrived at work I gave her the message. She read it and her face dropped. I quickly told her it was a joke and she laughed with us. One had finally been put over on her. She took it like a champ. I felt good. All those years of practical jokes against me and I finally pulled one off myself, successfully. Not bad for a beginner!

As I said before, never scam a scammer. The whole time I was setting this young lady up, she was working on me too. CPIC can be an extremely busy place. It's not out of the ordinary for the phones to be ringing, the radio going, CPIC messages coming in from outside agencies, people waiting, and on and on and on. It's also not uncommon for the women to come and go from the area for breaks, lunch, short deliveries of important paper and the like. I was working away and the flurry of activity began to increase. I took calls and stacked up the radio transmissions like an air traffic controller. I was going about my work when suddenly it dawned on me I was all by myself. I figured the ladies would be back soon so continued as best I could. The phone lines lit up like a Christmas tree. Car crews were calling in all at once and I was bouncing off the walls trying to keep up with everything.

I thought to myself, "Where the hell is everybody?"

A constable arrived from the Arrest

Processing Unit with some paperwork, while the intercom buzzed with a person from the back counter wanting a name run for warrants. That did it! I lost it!

I stood in the middle of the room and yelled at the top of my lungs, "Jesus, you're just going to have to wait!!!!"

Just as I threw my hands in the air I turned and there was all my staff, the inspector, the staff sergent and anyone else who was in the building at the time, grinning at me from the next room. I was had royally, yes, by the woman I had just caught earlier. Scammed by a scammer, I was.

**

Here are a few more odds and ends I thought you might like to relax with before we dive into the rest of the chapter.

A constable attended court and gave his testimony against the accused. After hearing all the evidence for the case, the judge found the man guilty and was about to pass sentence.

The accused, obviously in disagreement with the judge, vaulted from the prisoner's box and scaled the side of His Honour's bench in an attempt to attack him. The constable flew into action and leapt to the judge's rescue. He grabbed the accused, spun him around, and struck him in the face with his fist. The man fought back and was dragged from the bench by the constable. The officer placed him in a wrist lock, tumbled him up against the wall, handcuffed him and escorted him from the courtroom to the holding cell.

Out of the corner of his eye he noticed the judge making notes furiously. Moments later the constable returned to the court room and took a seat. The judge spoke:

"Constable, would you take the stand, please."

"Great," he thought, "I'm gonna get hell for saving his neck!"

He took the witness stand and faced the judge.

"It's my duty to inform you, constable, that no action of any type may be taken against a prisoner in the court room without my direct order. Is that clear?"

"Yes, Your Honour."

"Any action taken against an accused without my direct order can be construed as contempt of court. Is that clear?"

"Yes, Your Honour."

"Good! Now that we understand each other please follow these instructions retro-actively."

He read from his notes.

"Constable, grab the accused, spin him around and pull him from the bench. Now, constable, strike the accused in the face with your fist. Constable, place that man in a wrist lock and throw him against the wall. Put your hand-cuffs on the accused and escort him from the court room!"

"Yes, Your Honour."

"Well done, constable. You are very adept at following orders. You may step down."

"Thank you, Your Honour."

***

I was taking some CPIC papers to the Communications Centre one evening when I heard the following call come in.

"City Police."

"Hello, can you give me a definition of the word 'aggravated'?"

"In what context, sir?"

"As in assault, you know, aggravated assault?"

"Why don't you tell me what happened and I'll tell you if the circumstances qualify?"

"My neighbour keeps playing his stereo too loud. The sound assaults my ears and I get aggravated. Isn't that aggravated assault?"

"I'm sorry, sir, this is just a noise com-plaint. I'll send a car around to see you."

***

"City Police."

"Hi, I want to report a stolen car."

"Okay. What is the licence number of the vehicle?"

"It's 012345."

"You must be mistaken, sir. That plate number does not exist. Do you have the VIN number?"

"What's that?"

"The serial number of the vehicle, sir."

"It's 0A1234567C89."

"That number doesn't exist either, sir."

"Okay, try this one, 123ABC456DEF78."

"Yes, that one works. Your vehicle is a 1989 Toyota Corolla?"

"No."

"What does this VIN belong to then?"

"I don't know."

"Then why did you give it to me?"

"Well, you asked for a serial number and I don't have it so I just made that one up!"

***

Information came to us that a prolific bank robber was hiding in an apartment downtown. We drove to the building and the care taker let us in. He gave us the key and we

**"I THOUGHT THESE NEW CARS
WERE GONNA BE AIR CONDITIONED!"**

went up to the apartment with a warrant. The bad guy was reported armed and had fired a shot or two during the robberies, so we weren't about to take any chances. We opened the door very quietly and entered surreptitiously.

The shades in the apartment were drawn making it quite dark inside. We saw two figures in bed at the end of the hall. Not wanting him to get to his gun we raced down the hall and I leapt onto the bed yelling, "Police!"

He was arrested without much fuss at all.

The other person in the bed was his girlfriend. She got up naked and made no attempt to cover herself.

As my partner took the bad guy down the hall she looked at me with a smile and said, "Why don't you come and wake me up the same way tomorrow?"

I was lost for words.

***

Sometimes there's not a lot to do while you are on duty, and being the creative writer I am, I decided it was necessary to produce something. It was near Christmas and we were stuck in a lengthy traffic jam so I put pen to paper and came up with the following ditty:

THE CRIMINAL'S CHRISTMAS CAROL
(sung to the tune of Deck the Halls)
(with apologies to the composer)
by
Perry P. Rose

1) Rob the store and point the gun,
                Falalalalalalala
    Grab the cash I'm on the run,
                Falalalalalalala
    Tis the season to be stealing,
                Falalalalalalala
    What a rush 'o what a feeling.
                Falalalalalalala

2) Now I'll do some more shoplifting,
                Falalalalalalala
    Steal some presents - so uplifting
                Falalalalalalala
    So I'll go to court, big deal!
                Falalalalalalala
    Slap my wrist but I'll still steal.
                Falalalalalalala

3) Now the Tac Team's at my door,
                Falalalalalalala
    Knock me down upon the floor,
                Falalalalalalala
    That's okay, 'cause I'll complain,

Falalalalalalala

And I know it'll be sustained.

Falalalalalalala

4) Now I stand before the judge.

Falalalalalalala

Say police just have a grudge

Falalalalalalala

Whine and snivel - he believes me,

Falalalalalalala

Buys the line and then he frees me.

Falalalalalalala

5) Back to work I go once more,

Falalalalalalala

Steal a car and rob a store,

Falalalalalalala

If they chase me I won't stop,

Falalalalalalala

I'll outrun the city cops.

Falalalalalalala

6) Now I race into the country,

Falalalalalalala

City cops call out the Mounties.

Falalalalalalala

Now I know that I'm in shit,

Falalalalalalala

Here they come and I'll get hit!

Falalalalalalala

7)   Through the car headfirst I go,
                    Falalalalalalalala
    Lip stand on the ice and snow,
                    Falalalalalalalala
    Wrap my head around a post,
                    Falalalalalalalala
    Chase is over I'm a ghost!
                    Falalalalalalalala

***

Once upon a time a young man worked in an office. There was a particularly beautiful secretary who worked there also. Over the months the young man became obsessed. He wanted very much to go to bed with her. One day he left a note on her desk, but, alas, she ignored it. Relentless, the misguided fellow accosted the lady outside the building after work. He groped her private parts to which she understandably objected. He was subsequently arrested and charged with sexual assault.

The groper plead not guilty and the case went to trial by judge and jury. The note he had left on her desk was a crucial piece of evidence. The investigating officer had seized it and brought it to court.

The secretary took the witness stand and the prosecutor asked her numerous questions.

He then produced the note and held it in front of her.

"And then," he asked, "the accused gave you this note, did he not?"

"Yes," she replied.

At this time the judge leaned forward and asked to read the note. The prosecutor passed it to him and he read it to himself. It contained the words written very plainly, "I'd like to have sex with you."

In a moment he passed it back, saying, "I think the jury should read this as well."

The court clerk took the note and gave it to the jury foreman who read it and passed it on. So it went down the front row of the jury with each member reading the contents. The last juror in the front row passed it to the lady behind him and she read the contents. When she went to pass it to the old fellow sitting next to her she noticed that he was sleeping. With a gentle nudge, she woke him and passed him the note.

The old fellow opened the paper and read the contents. With a gasp he quickly folded the paper and stuffed it into his suit pocket.

The judge was watching this and asked, "You there, what are you doing?"

The old fellow sat bolt upright, "Nothing, My Lord."

"No, no. The note man, what are you doing with that note?" the judge pressed.

"That, sir," said the old juror, "is a personal matter between this young lady and my-self."

***

We had a sergeant who was very nervous about everything. His habit was to twirl a match stick between his thumbs while he was sitting at the desk. There was never much for him to do, but when he put the match stick down you knew he was going to do something ridiculous as usual.

Our old police building had a window in the sergeant's office that provided a view of the main street. As a matter of fact it was immediately adjacent to the main street. One day, as he was sitting at his desk with not much to do, a huge tanker truck pulled up and stopped right outside the window. The cab was directly opposite the glass panes, and the front portion of the huge aluminum tank was just visible. As the sergeant watched in horror, the driver took out a package of tobacco and started to roll a cigarette. Our leader dropped his match stick, which was the first sign, and bolted out the front door. When he reached the cab the guy was just licking the paper. The sergeant yarded the door open and grabbed the cigarette from the poor guy's hand.

"You fool," he yelled, crushing the cigarette to pulp. "A single spark from your cigarette could ignite this whole truck!"

The driver leaned out the door and pointed back at the tank.

"Are you nuts, fella," he shouted, "I'm haulin' milk."

***

Littering is a pet peeve of mine. I put my garbage in garbage cans and I expect others to do the same. I was driving my police car down the main drag one day when I saw a guy take the last bite from a burger he was eating and toss the wrapper onto the grass boulevard. He also dropped his milkshake cup and takeout bag.

I was not impressed! I pulled the car to the side of the road and rolled down my window.

"Hey," I yelled, "Come here!"

He did.

"What do you think you're doing tossing your garbage around for someone else to clean up? I want you to pick all that stuff up right now and put it into a garbage can."

The guy leaned into the window with a definite attitude and yelled back at me, "I don't see any garbage can around here, do you?"

Without thinking I yelled back, "Listen fella, I have to take a shit but I don't see a

toilet around, so am I gonna use the boulevard?"

"Your choice," he said, walking away.

***

The railroad crossing arm was down and
a train was approaching slowly. About four
drivers facing us decided they could beat the
train and drove around the barricade. My
partner and I jumped out of our car quickly
and flagged over the offenders. The last
vehicle was an older van and I signalled the
driver to pull over to the curb. I was dealing
with the drivers in order and as I walked to
the first car I heard heavy acceleration behind
me. The van was fleeing.

I tossed my summons folder to my partner and jumped into the police car to give
chase. This guy really wanted to get away.
He drove down the first street and into an
alley. As I turned into the alley I could just
see his brake lights turning onto the next
street. So it went for about fifteen blocks. At
one point I lost sight of him and a citizen
pointed to the next alley where he was just
leaving again. It was one of the wildest chases
I had ever been in. The cars bounced out of
the alleys and the dust flew and the tires
squealed, just like on TV.

I finally managed to get him stopped

"THE GUY THAT HIT ME WAS ..."

right back at the alley where my partner was still writing tickets. The van slid to a halt because the alley was blocked by another vehicle. I jumped out of the police car and with adrenalin pumping I ran to the driver's door of the vehicle. I flung the door open and reached inside to grasp the dastardly offender. I came up with two handfuls of one of the oldest gentlemen I have ever had the misfortune to meet. I mean this guy had to be pushing ninety-nine years.

He was laughing and slapping his leg and didn't even flinch when I took hold of him.

He finally managed to blurt out, "Heh, heh, heh ... all these years o' drivin' an' I always wanted to do thet ... Gimme the ticket sonny ... it were werth it ... heh, heh, heh."

"Sheeeshh!" was all I could come back with.

***

A car crew called for back-up with an impaired driver. We responded. When we got there we saw the officers inside their car and a drunk leaning up against the fender. We couldn't see what the problem was, but we figured we'd take this guy into custody and then talk to the car crew about what they wanted done with him.

I stepped out of the car and said to the guy, "Step over here."

"Why?" he asked.

"Because I want to talk to you," I said.

"Fuck you," he said, and I took exception to this.

I reached out and grabbed him. The fight was on. He struggled and kicked. I twisted and punched. He spit and stomped. I cursed and grunted. I finally managed to get him handcuffed and into the rear seat of our police car. As fast as I put him in one side he slid across the seat and went out the other door. This guy was wiry.

We eventually had to tie his feet to his wrists and lay him on the back seat to stop him from kicking the doors and breaking the windows. Now I understood why the other car crew had called for backup - this guy was a maniac!

I put my tie back on and refastened the buttons on my shirt as I walked to the other police car.

The driver rolled down the window and said, "That was some scrap. What you bustin' him for?"

"What do you mean?" I asked. "That's your impaired driver. What do you want us to do with him?"

"I don't think so," said the constable. "This is our guy here in our car."

"Well, who the hell was that?" I asked, rubbing a sore spot on my chin.

"I dunno," he said. "He was just leaning up against our car when you got here. I never saw him before."

"Wonderful," I said. "Just bloody wonderful."

***

Being a rookie can be as difficult as working with one. My first week on the job we were sent to retrieve a drunk from a restaurant, where we found a guy, semi-comatose, at a table. We gathered him up and took him outside, all the while not bothering to be too cautious, because he appeared to be very, very drunk. Just when we tried to stuff him into the back of the paddy wagon, he twisted out of our grip and ran. He was rather adept for someone who had had that much to drink and my partner and I were both out of breath by the time we recaptured him. Off we took our prize to the van. and this time, with greater caution, placed him into the rear caged area. He refused to tell us his name so we began searching his belongings to find some ID. My partner climbed into the back of the van with him and I crawled in following my senior officer's lead like a good little rookie. I shut the door.

"What did you do?" my officer coach asked me.

"I didn't want this guy to run again so I closed the door. Is something wrong?" I replied.

"No," he said, rolling his eyes up into his head, "but when you figure out just how the hell we're going to get out of here, would you mind letting me in on the secret!"

It was only then I realized with horror there was no handle on the inside of the cage door.

There we were, captive and captors, stuck in the paddy wagon with a drunk. We didn't want to call on the radio and tell every cop in the city we were locked in the back of our own paddy wagon with a drunk, we wouldn't live it down for years. So, we did the next best and obviously most well-thought-out thing we could come up with, we started banging on the windows and yelling at the people who were passing by.

An old guy came by and looked in. We tried to show him our shoulder flashes but he just ignored us and left. A lady walking her cat refused to even look at the van which was rocking back and forth violently with the force of our thumping. A police car drove by and we immediately ceased all activity. As soon as it disappeared around the corner we started thumping and yelling again. We were in there about half an hour before someone finally had mercy on us and let us out. We swore him to secrecy immediately. I felt an inch high and my senior officer wanted to kick me sky high. Can't say that I blame him.

***

I went to a family dispute one night where a lady had been accidentally knocked out by her friend's husband. He had taken a swing at someone, missed, and hit his wife's friend in the jaw, knocking her out cold. When we got there everyone was talking at once like a scene from a "B" grade comedy, and we couldn't make any sense out of it.

While all this was going on, the family dog was running back and forth, back and forth, making an annoying clicking sound with his teeth. I couldn't stand it any longer so I picked up the damned dog.

I looked into his mouth and asked, "Does your dog have false teeth?"

The woman jumped with a yell, "Oh, thank God you found them! I saw them fly out of Judy's mouth when she got hit. We've looked everywhere for them."

She grabbed the teeth from my hand and rubbed them once or twice on the side of her dress. Bending over her friend she pulled her jaw open and slid the teeth back in. " W e just won't say anything when she wakes up. It'll be all right."

***

Sunday night shift is boring. Nothing happens, and by four o'clock in the morning you're going stir crazy. We met another car crew in an industrial area and played a few games of hide n' seek with them. After about an hour we tired of that and decided to go to a restaurant for coffee.

As we neared the main drag, which was deserted, my partner said to me, "Slow down and let the other guys catch up. I'm gonna hang a moon at them."

He undid his pants and slid them down. Just as we reached the main intersection he hung his butt out the window. I changed lanes and left a space between the police cars. Out of nowhere came a taxi with four passengers and the damn thing pulled right in between us. They certainly got a close-up view of the full moon with my partner's ass hanging out the window. I hit the emergency lights and we got the hell out of there.

***

When you are a rookie, you respond to every call with a sense of urgency. I was working with a very senior partner who had learned to take it slow, and never moved at more than a snail's pace.

We were dispatched to a break and enter in progress and my adrenalin was pumping. By the time he pulled up at the house I was in high gear and bolted from the car. My partner got out slowly, reached for his hat, and began strolling across the front lawn of the residence.

As I sprang from the car the seatbelt strap wrapped around my gun butt and tied itself into a knot. I was going at full tilt, ramming my hat onto my head at the same time. Before I knew it the belt tightened and I reached the end of my rope. It twisted me around and I slammed heavily against the side of the car. My hat went flying and I was badly winded. As I was trying desperately to extricate myself I noticed my partner looking over his shoulder at me shaking his head.

"No wonder they call you rookies!" he said.

"MY BACK NEVER FELT BETTER ...
HOW'D YA DO IT DOC!!"

CHAPTER NINE

"Rookie" defined as a raw recruit. Ah yes, the shiny-faced constable, the freshly-pressed, not a spot on it uniform, the gleaming boots, the wide-eyed glazed look of someone who plans to save the world from crime and stem the tides of communist aggression.

Rookies are sent by their officer coaches to the CPIC area where they pick up paperwork to finish processing arrests. Usually they have no idea why they are there, so now it is our turn for a little fun.

"Guess what, ladies, we have a new kid on the block!"

The scene: a young radiant face arrives at the CPIC counter. You can always tell who they are, not only by the fact that you could cut your fingers on the creases in their uniforms, but by the way they ask for what it is their senior partner sent them to pick up. They don't have a clue! They don't want to appear like they didn't learn a damn thing in the Academy so they hit you up with nonsensical small talk for fifteen minutes. They ramble on and on (not about vasectomies yet, that's for the older guys) and then slip in the question. "And while I'm here have you got a warrant for so and so?"

"So, you're here to pick up the warrant," I say, handing the control form to the rookie. (Attached to the warrant is a form which has to be signed by the officer executing the warrant. The control form is supposed to stay in CPIC.) Down the hall he goes with his prize and what he figures is the paperwork.

Of course, rookies also hate to ask basic questions like, "Is this the piece of paper I need to complete the job?"

God forbid he should prove to the ladies in CPIC he doesn't know anything even though he's only been on since lunch and it is now five in the afternoon.

Of course, the dinosaurs (anyone who has been on the force more than ten years) like nothing better than watching their charges squirm a little. Why not? They've survived to tell us all these stories. Some may even stoop to setting a rookie up! Never, you say? Read on!

One rookie answered a phone at the district office. After finishing the call he noticed what he thought was purple ink on his hand and went to wash it off. As he scrubbed away the purple colour started spreading instead of fading. He quickly wiped his hands and face with a paper towel. Now it was all over him, into his moustache and even on his teeth. The joker had even put the "miracle powder" on the paper towels. Needless to say this young fellow had to take the day off and go home to scrub down with Comet cleanser and a scouring pad. Purple teeth, face and moustache wouldn't go over well in the Court of Queen's Bench where he had to appear the next day.

Rookies also do their jobs with a lot of aplomb and enthusiasm. One day a rookie and his partner were near a fresh robbery. When the suspect's vehicle description was circulated, they came upon it and, after a short chase, stopped the fleeing car. The rookie, wanting to show his stuff, raced to the curb side of the vehicle and yanked the passenger out. His training took over and he began the search for weapons. Up and down and all over the suspect he searched, legs, waist band, arms ... breasts?

Suddenly jumping back he yelled, "Christ, its a girl!"

He threw his hands into the air and walked back to the police car, muttering, "Holy shit, that's a girl! Holy shit, that's a girl! We're not supposed to search women like that. I'm done for!"

Hopefully by now he can tell the difference.

Before we continue, a few more interesting stories from the Comm. Centre.

***

"City Police, can I help you?"

"I just got attacked by the Granny from Hell!"

"I beg your pardon?"

"Yeah, I was on the bike path and this old lady rode up to me. She jumped off her bike, yelled at me, shoved me, and spit at me."

"I see, sir."

"I just want you to warn everybody to stay off the bike path!"

"We'll look after it, sir."

***

"City Police."

"Hi, I have a strange drunk passed out in my yard. I'm having a bar-b-que tonight and I didn't invite him. Will you send someone to pick him up or should I just toss him over the fence into the alley?

***

This call was dispatched as is: Domestic dispute. Complainant needs help removing her clothing.

Guess how many cars volunteered for that one!

***

On minor complaints we take the calls and then call the victim back to do the report over the phone when we have time. I called a guy back who wanted to report a carprowling. This was the conversation:

"Hello, sir. This is the City Police calling you back to take your report."

"What report?"

"Did you call this morning and say your car had been broken into?"

"Yes."

"Okay, I'll take the report from you now."

"But I already called the police."

"That's why I'm calling you back, sir ... to take the report."

"What report?"

"The police report, sir."

"Well, who the hell are you?"

"I'm the police."

"I already called the police."

"I know that, sir. I want to take the report."

"Oh, you want to go over and wait by the car then?"

"No. I'll take the report over the phone."

"What report?"

"Forget it, sir. I'll send a car crew over to see you."

As you can see, learning is a continuous experience on the street. So, let's continue learning more about our knights in blue armour. Ready?

***

One day my partner and I were at a pedestrian accident. We interviewed and took a statement from one of the witnesses. My partner was reading the statement out loud. "Blah, blah, blah, this happened and then the 'presbyterian' stepped into the cross-walk ..."

For some reason he didn't make the connection that the witness meant "pedestrian", so he turned to the guy and asked, "How did you know he was a Presbyterian?"

"Because he was in the cross-walk," he said.

"How does that make him a Presbyterian?"

I started to laugh. Trying not to be obvious, tears running down my face, I got out of the car so they wouldn't see me. By now my partner was getting a little perturbed at this witness because they were disagreeing with each other.

"This guy in the cross-walk may not be a

AQUARIUS --
THE WATER CARRIER

Presbyterian."

The witness persisted, "But he is because he was in the cross-walk."

The nickel dropped, along with my partner's face. He made a speedy retreat from the car, gut-laughing as he went. Finally, the witness made the connection and he too got out of the car, laughing hysterically. We must have made quite a scene at an injury accident.

**

I was not new on the job, but new enough to still feel a little bit intimidated by people. One day I was working alone and had to deliver a subpoena to a downtown restaurant. This establishment was usually frequented by a group of what I would describe as local persons who are not too enamoured with the police. As I drove up they never took their eyes off me. I walked into the restaurant looking straight ahead, delivered the subpoena, and walked out. I knew, I just knew, that if they continued to stare at me I was going to do something rookieish.

I finally made it outside praying all the while I wouldn't trip on the sidewalk or bump into a fire hydrant. God help me that I should lose this facade of being a very self-assured, experienced and otherwise seasoned policeman.

I opened the car door and slipped in with a sigh of relief. As I reached for the steering wheel I realized I was sitting in the back seat.

***

I had only been on the street for about fifteen weeks. I was assigned Check Stop duty and along came my first customer driving a van. I signalled the driver like I was supposed to and the van stopped. Inside were two lovely young ladies, smiling all over the place.

I went into my practiced spiel, "How are you ladies this evening? Could I please see your particulars?"

The lady in the driver's seat looked at the passenger and they both grinned.

I asked again, "Could I please see your particulars?" The driver reached into her purse and pulled out a pair of lacy, red panties, the kind that look like a thong.

She asked, "How are these for particulars?"

I was absolutely speechless. After about five seconds of staring at the panties I said, "I don't think those are exactly the particulars I'm looking for."

She said, "Well, that's too bad," and snaked them through her fingers and dropped them back into her purse.

The Academy sure didn't tell me what the hell to say in this sort of situation.

***

It was a cold, rainy Sunday morning, and I was assigned to motorcycle duty. Seven or eight of us met at the police garage and mounted up for the shift. We were supposed to work the south of the city for the morning, but we all agreed that it was a little too miserable to stand out in the rain and write tickets. Someone came up with a brilliant idea. We all rode off to a large park in the southwest area, and when we arrived it was deserted.

We found a picnic shelter and pulled our bikes inside. A bunch of us gathered up as many picnic tables as we could find and blocked out the rain. We stuck them into the windows and door to keep ourselves dry until the storm passed. One of the guys had a deck of cards so we got into a few games. I had a thermos of coffee. We were prepared for the worst.

Time passed and we suddenly realized it was noon. I peeked out through a crack in the tables. To my horror the sun was out and the park was filled with people. We put the cards away and mounted up. With a great roar we started our bikes inside the shelter, and I removed the picnic table from the door. Bike after bike filed out into the sunlight. The picnickers stopped and stared in disbelief.

As I exited the shed someone asked me, "What's going on?"

"Nothing," I said. "It's a secret tunnel from the police garage, now don't tell anyone, okay."

***

Fingerprints of suspects are taken at headquarters. They make an appointment and then we take the pictures and print them. One day a lady came in ready to be processed. In order to ensure that we get a proper print the hands must be clean of all foreign substances. We have a sink and soap available in the corner of the room.

In my usual business tones I said to the woman, "You can wash over there," and pointed to the sink.

I went about my work filling out the papers and waited for her. She seemed to be taking an unusually long time so I walked over to see what the problem was. There she was with her head stuck in the sink and her hair lathered up with suds.

"What the hell are you doing?" I asked.

"What you told me, washing my hair," she replied.

"No, no, I said WASH OVER THERE!"

***

We got a call one night to an older part of town on a sudden death. We rolled up in front of the house to find an older gentleman, quite intoxicated, standing on the sidewalk. He told us his wife had died and was laying in bed. My partner stayed with him and I went in to confirm the death. It was a smaller house with a tiny bedroom. The lighting consisted of one bare bulb suspended from the ceiling in the kitchen and one in the bedroom thath didn't work at all.

I lit my flashlight and walked into the tiny room, trying not to fall over the bed as I did. It was really cramped. There she was, laying on the bed, face up, covered, and not a breath coming out of her that I could see in the dim light.

I worked my way around to the far side of the bed and leaned over to pull the covers down. I was going to check for pulse or heat to determine how long ago the poor lady had expired. As I snapped the covers away the woman sat bolt upright in bed and screamed. I fell back against the wall and screamed too!

224

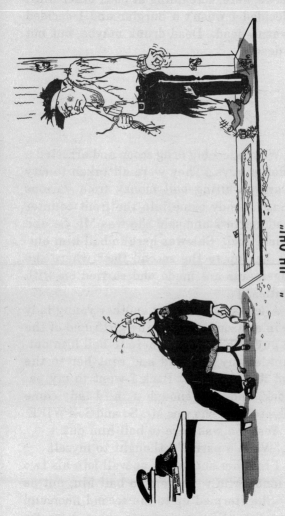

"... UH-OH!"

(IF YOU DON'T GET THIS REFER TO PAGE 155)

There we were, screaming at each other until she decided I wasn't a burglar and I decided she wasn't dead. Dead drunk maybe, but not dead dead.

***

We made a big drug scoop and arrested a half dozen guys. They were all taken to city cells and awaiting bail money from various sources. A lady came into the front counter at headquarters and said she was Mr. So and So's girlfriend. She was here to bail him out. I sent her up to the second floor where the arrangements are made and carried on with my duties.

A few minutes later another young lady came in and said she was the girlfriend of the same guy. She also was here to bail him out. I wrinkled my forehead and sent her to the second floor as well. Back I went to my paperwork, and sure enough a third lady came in. She told me she was Mr. So and So's WIFE.

Yes, she was here to bail him out.

"What a party!" I thought to myself.

I told her she might as well join his two girlfriends who were here to bail him out as well. She stormed up to the second floor and in moments the three women came down together ... without Mr. So and So.

***

One night as I was leaving the front door of headquarters, I stumbled over a Native Indian who had had a little too much to drink and was passed out in the foyer. I roused him and said, "Come on, you gotta get out of here before the chief gets here."

He looked up at me and said, "The chief doesn't even know I'm here. He thinks I'm still on the reserve."

"Not your chief, mine," I said, helping him to his feet and escorting him out.

***

I have a secret desire to be a member of the TAC team and my hero is Spiderman. We had to affect an arrest one day in an apartment building and we decided to do it a little differently. The bad guy was a known runner and we didn't want to be chasing him any farther than we had too.

I told my partner to keep an eye on the front door while I found a way up to the balcony. The building was very close to the next door structure, so I went up onto the roof and looked down into the adjacent apartment ...

nine stories up. I judged the distance and knew I could jump from the roof onto the guy's balcony. I would then make the arrest before he knew what hit him, just like Spiderman.

I picked my target. With a great spring I leapt from the rooftop and landed with a tremendous crash on the balcony. There was a girl sitting on the couch watching TV, and she screamed bloody murder.

"What the hell are you doing on my balcony?"

"Oops!" I said with a strained grin. "You're not going to believe this, but I have the wrong apartment. Excuse me!"

I slinked across the divider onto the next balcony and peered in through the glass. I could hear movement and pressed my face closer for a view. There I saw another woman, stark naked ... cooking breakfast. (God I hope I got the right one this time!)

I waited a moment and then the guy we wanted came out of the bedroom, naked as well. He slumped down on the couch as I stepped into full view.

I pulled back the patio door and stated quite professionally, "You're under arrest."

Without batting an eye, he replied, "Well, just let me get some clothes."

He disappeared into the bedroom, and in seconds was running bare balls, with clothes in hand out the roof entrance. Just like vanishing cream ... gone.

Tales from the Police Locker room Vol. I

That never happens to Spiderman!

"A CONSTABLE'S LIFE NEVER CHANGES."

EPILOGUE

Have we left any portion of the Police Service unscathed? If we have it's only because we ran out of room. Day by day your crime fighters hit the pavement (sometimes literally) to go forth and test their mettle. Pressed and polished these macho or machess officers take to the streets and somehow manage to preserve the image. Amid the unzipped flies, stunt falls from radar cars, and lenses falling from sunglasses, they push ever onward to preserve the myth.

Civilians continue to believe in the myth. Let's face it, you can tell a man of steel by the rust on his underwear and how he suffered through his vasectomy. I, Joan, have suffered right along with you. During the trips out to Perry's home I have asked myself many times, "Where is a policeman when you need one?" Having written this manuscript I'm sure we all know by now. I have had to take the busiest freeway in order to get to his place, and usually in rush hour traffic. I have been cut off, honked at, tailgated, and passed on the right!!!! I seem to have put my life on the line, carrying my precious cargo of stories, as much as the policeman out on the street. But it has been worth it, every last life-threatening moment.

Well, Joan, I agree with you. I have glued the lenses back into my sunglasses and I never approach a car now without giving my fly the one finger, over the belt, check to see if it's done up.

So, the next time you see that police car flitting through traffic like a gnat on a summer's night, you will have first-hand knowledge of what is really taking place inside. He may be trying to unwrap the microphone cord from the steering wheel, untangle his bootlaces from the shotgun rack, or balancing a slurpy while doing both. If you look closely, you may be able to see his hands darting over the equipment rack with alleged expertise as he tries to turn on the siren without dumping his drink or running off the road. When you see all this, remember above all ... smile ... you may be in the next book.

One final story to leave you with:

The sports car zipped in and out of traffic tailgating, speeding, and making unnecessary lane changes.

I walked on the accelerator of the police cruiser and quickly caught up to the offender.

He pulled over and as I stepped from the car I noticed he was a very, very large man in a very, very small sports car.

"You're being stopped for speeding," I informed him.

"Can I explain, officer?"

"You can try."

"My wife thinks it's macho for me to have this damned sports car. As you can see I'm really too big to be in here. The seats are so bloody small that when I drive my penis falls asleep ... so I have to speed to get where I'm going!"

WE WANT YOUR STORIES

As long as there are police officers, paramedics and fire fighters, there will be hilarious stories to tell about their misadventures. We want to hear from you for our next book. If you have funny anecdotes about any of these professions please type them on paper or record them on a standard-sized audio cassette and forward them to:

WORDSTORM PRODUCTIONS INC.,
P.O. BOX 49132, 7740 - 18 STREET S.E.,
CALGARY, ALBERTA
CANADA T2C 3W5

Phone / Fax: (403) 236 -1275   Email: wordstrm@cadvision.com

FOR OUR U.S. CUSTOMERS PLEASE CONTACT

WORDSTORM PRODUCTIONS INC.,
1520 3 rd. St. NW. C104,
GREAT FALLS, MONTANA,
USA 59404

ABOUT THE AUTHORS

PERRY P. ROSE

Perry was born in Toronto, Ontario, the son of a Canadian Armed Forces Sergeant. The uniform has been no stranger to Perry throughout his life. He holds a Teaching Certificate for the Province of Ontario and moved to Calgary in 1970 while performing as a professional musician. He is a published songwriter with eight songs to his credit, a published freelance writer with articles in Central Coast Parent, The Call Box, 10-4 Magazine and The Olympian. Perry has also published a children's musical for the Calgary Police Service called "Stranger Danger", a puppet show to teach children the dangers of the street. He has also been the editor of two monthly newsletters, The Six Pack and The Southeast Reformer. He began collecting stories with Joan in 1988 and the result was the manuscript which you have just read. Perry is still serving as a Constable with the Calgary Police Service as he has since 1982.

JOAN NELSON

Joan was born in Gilbert Plains, Manitoba. After completing her schooling and receiving certification as a clerk typist she commenced work with the Royal Canadian Mounted Police in Grande Cache, Alberta, as a stenographer. Developing a love for the civilian side of Police work, Joan moved on to the R.C.M.P. detachment at St. Albert, Alberta, where she worked as a dispatcher. She finally moved to Calgary where she has worked for the past sixteen years as a C.P.I.C. supervisor. Joan began collecting stories shortly after arriving in Calgary and since then has become a self-educated researcher.

ORDERING INFORMATION

Tales from the Police Locker room Vols. I & II

make excellent gifts for anyone.

To order in Canada please send cheque or money order in Canadian funds to:

WORDSTORM PRODUCTIONS INC.
PO BOX 49132, 7740 - 18 ST. SE,
CALGARY, ALBERTA, CANADA T2C 3W5

$9.95 + $3.50 (shipping and handling) +
$.94 (GST) = $14.39

To order in the United States please send cheque or money order in U.S. funds to:

WORDSTORM PRODUCTIONS INC.,
1520 - 3 ST NW, C-104,
GREAT FALLS, MONTANA, USA
59404

$9.95 + $3.50 (shipping and handling) =
$13.45

Tales from the Police Locker room Vol. II

PERRY P. ROSE

Trial by comedy continues!!! A motorist is accused by his own lawyer of driving a pencil! The macho Tactical Weapons team pepper sprays themselves instead of the bad guys! Police are in hot persuit of a "Veal Cutlet".

The zany antics of police and criminals from around the world are captured in this volume of side-splitting stories. Previously known as "Blue-pers", this book received **TOP GOLD** AWARD from Brandi Jasmine's Internet Review.

ISBN 0-9697756-6-0

304pp/50 illustrations

Retail Price $9.95

See order page in this book for ordering instructions